FLIM FLAM
MAN
A LEGACY OF LIES

by JIM PUGH

authorHOUSE®

AuthorHouse™
1663 Liberty Drive
Bloomington, IN 47403
www.authorhouse.com
Phone: 1 (800) 839-8640

Published by AuthorHouse   10/06/2015

ISBN: 978-1-5049-4973-6 (sc)
ISBN: 978-1-5049-4972-9 (e)

Print information available on the last page.

Any people depicted in stock imagery provided by Thinkstock are models, and such images are being used for illustrative purposes only.
Certain stock imagery © Thinkstock.

This book is printed on acid-free paper.

The First Year of Obama

When Barack Obama was inaugurated in 2009, he became the first African American to hold the office of President of the United States. All through his long campaign he had told us what he was going to do to correct all the mistakes of George W. Bush during the eight years previous. He also told us over and over again just how he was going to change the "political culture of this nation as we know it."

He failed to do that as he failed in just about every other thing he promised the nation. What follows is a groups of columns I wrote for the Benicia Herald and the Vallejo Times Herald in California in 2009.

I hope you will find them educational and interesting, as well as unsettling and disturbing.

Jim Pugh

2009 Titles:

The Oval Office-A Union Hall?

Net Neutrality. What?

What Did You Say Mr. Robinson?

Safety is Our Priority

The EPA Power Grab

A Series of Unfortunate Events

Within the last few months, politics have gone sour on our President. According to "Murphy's Law". If it can get worse, it will. And in regard to Barrack Obama, it has. The odd part of all this is the fact that this President does not seem to realize or really care much if it does or not.

Recently, Obama has let it be known that he is not all that much concerned if he gets reelected. That is an astounding statement by a President that has been in office less than 2 years of his first term. According to Politico.com, the President had an agenda when first elected in 2008 and he feels that he has achieved a great deal of what he proposed. Although a majority of the politically savvy would dare to differ.

It appears that the lower the President goes in the polls, the more positive attention he is given by the mainstream media. It is as if he is a little boy given a pat on the head by a loving nanny every time he does a no-no. In his case, it is a big, big hug and kiss. But, let's face it folks, this President has failed at just about everything he has attempted to do in his first 2 years. The one huge bill he was able to force feed down the throats of the American people (Healthcare) is extremely unpopular and continues to be a negative example of what our government can do and will do…regardless of the way the average American feels about it.

The total disregard for the well being of our citizens living on the Mexican-Arizona border is just another example of the President burning another bridge. From a purely political stand point, this President has little or no chance of carrying the State of Arizona in 2012, if he continues down this road of total abandonment of the American citizens on the border.

The cynical say that it is all about the votes. Those ten million Hispanic votes that will surely go to Obama and the Democratic Party should the President's "Immigration Reform" go through Congress. And really…how can anyone with a clear head and half a brain not see this as a strategy in place in the Obama White House. Just look at what is going on all around us and it is hard to deny there is an agenda and it is wreaking havoc on the American people and the President is aware of it.

Big in the press this past week has been the Michelle Obama pleasure trip to Spain with one daughter and several close friends. This was a trip that cost the American taxpayer over one half million dollars. Even the Presidents Chief of Staff, David Axlerod, had a near heart attack when first told of this. According to the Huffington Post, there was quite a blow up in the Oval Office with four letter words flying everywhere. Would it be fair to say that this President and his wife are totally tone deaf when it comes to taking elite vacations in foreign countries and American resorts of the rich and famous, while the beautiful resorts of the Gulf Coast are suffering a terrible disaster on their lovely beaches? Do you think it would be considered whining if they had less than pleasant things to say about it?

On the East Coast, the press is full of news regarding a Muslim group' attempt to build a Mosque on (or near) the site of the Twin Towers disaster. This, of course, has the clear approval of the President (no big surprise there) but what is surprising is the support of some big time Republican politicians like Michael Bloomberg, the Mayor of New York City and Jerry Nadler, (D-NY). As it regards Nadler, nothing is too surprising, but Bloomberg...I will have to admit..that one did catch me off guard. But, not only did the President support the Inman attempting to build the Mosque, he has actually named the man to represent this country at a large Muslim gathering in the Middle East next month.

Excuse me? Could someone please explain the reasoning behind that move? I have to admit, when it comes to this President and his actions as they regard anything Muslim, I am at a total loss. And that brings us back to the start of the article. It simply doesn't register with this man that most of the things that he is doing as President lately do not cause a positive reaction on behalf of the American electorate. Is he playing "Chicken" with the American voter, then he is most likely a one term President. From his actions lately, I would assume that was just what he expects Go figure.

The Error of Obama

I truly believe that there is something driving our current president that is not in the best interest of this country. I am not saying that Barrack Obama is anything but a patriotic American, but what I am saying is this president has much less regard for his own country than he absolutely must have to be the quality of leader we so need at this time.

Seven days after his inauguration speech. He delivered another speech, this one to the Muslim world reassuring worldwide Muslims that "we are not your enemy". The seemingly urgent timing of that message was odd and actually disturbing. In reality, we are not at war with Islam. We have never been at war with the Muslim religion. We are at war with a group of religious terrorists who happen to be Muslim.

Since his election, Obama has continued to characterize America as a very guilty nation. America, according to the president, is guilty of arrogance, greed, and just about every other sin under the sun, but none worse than insufficient respect for Muslims. Could someone please explain this conduct to me? Could someone please tell me why our President deems it necessary to bow and kiss the ring of a Saudi King, but not to show the same respect to the Queen of England? Actually, I don't think our Presidents, regardless of who they are, should bow to any other ruler on this earth.

I would say this to this president that yes, WE ARE AT WAR with the enemies of this country regardless of who they are. And no, we do not have any more of an obligation to kneel to the King of Saudi Arabia than we do to any other sovereign ruler. This is the strongest, most generous, and fairest nation on this planet. It is a shame that our president doesn't seem to believe that. And to those Muslims who are killing Americans in Afghanistan and Iraq, I would say this- we are your enemy.

This president has shown much more enthusiasm to take on cable news than to attack Muslim terrorism in the Middle East. That is not an opinion folks. That is an absolute fact. I wrote a previous column that Obama was not in a hurry to make a decision in regards to a troop increase in Afghanistan. That was a while back and he hasn't proved me wrong.

On September 16, 2001, President George Bush, while speaking to the White House reporters spoke these words, "people have declared war on America and they have made a terrible mistake…my administration has a job to do and we are going to do it. We will rid the world of the evil doers". Can anyone imagine our current President saying the same words? I can, but with this addition…unless they are Muslims.

EPA Cap and Trade Regulation- no sense at all

Last year I wrote columns in regard to the Environmental Protection Agency and its attempt to regulate greenhouse emission using any methods at its' disposal. On the 7th of this month, Congressional Republicans passed a bill that prevents the EPA from regulating greenhouse emissions. Also on this day, Senate Majority leader Harry Reid successfully maneuvered to prevent passage of the same legislation in the Senate sponsored by Minority Leader Mitch McConnell (R-Ky). The bills were nearly identical. Congressional Republicans are trying to stop the Obama administration's EPA from continuing to implement new regulations that tax businesses and raise gas prices in order to pursue its climate change agenda. The EPA is using the Clean Air Act (CAA) as a vehicle for its new Cap and Trade regulations (or as some have called it…its Cap and Tax regulations).

The White House has released a veto threat of the house bill, Energy Tax Prevention Act (HR 910) two days before it was voted on the floor. EPA regulations of carbon dioxide emissions that come from coal, oil, and natural gas raise the energy cost of consumers, which trickles down to increase the cost of everything from gasoline to groceries.

This president and his party are absolutely dedicated to force the regulation of greenhouse emissions through the Environmental Protection Agency. We all know that this administration wanted a Cap and Trade system to regulate greenhouse gases, but the Congress said no. So beginning in early 2009, EPA began putting together a house of cards to regulate emissions of carbon dioxide.

Despite Obama's veto threat, the Energy Tax Prevention Act passed the House by a vote of 255 to 172 with 19 Democrats voting for it. This bill would block the EPA from using the CAA to create new regulations that curb greenhouse gases and impose a backdoor energy tax. It is an obvious travesty of justice that this government is deliberately imposing politics that will harm job creators and working families…and what for? The EPA's

Administrator (Lisa Jackson herself) admits U.S. regulation of greenhouse gases will NOT affect global climate conditions.

As Democrats were unable to pass Cap and Trade in the previous Congress, this bill prohibits the Obama administration from regulating what it could not legislate. The Administration strongly opposes House passage of HR190, which would halt the EPA's common sense steps under the Clean Air Act to protect Americans from harmful air pollution. HR910 would also increase the nation's dependence on oil and other fossil fuels as well. Democrats themselves recognize the dangers of these EPA regulations. Yet instead of just voting for that one amendment that solves the problem they're hiding behind sham amendments designed to give them political cover. None of the four EPA amendments got enough votes to pass...which was Harry Reid's plan from inception.

These Cap and Trade policies have been pushed by Congressional Democrats and the president for almost two years. The House Democrats passed Cap and Trade by seven votes in 2009 but to the eternal shame of Barbara Boxer, the bill died in the Senate. As the Republicans were about to take control of the House this past December, the Obama White House instituted new EPA regulations to put Cap and Trade policies into effect Obama's EPA used the CAA as a vehicle for the new regulation, which imposes a tax in the form of carbon emissions to businesses to regulate their greenhouse gasses. The agency began with automobiles, declaring that their emissions endangered public health and welfare. That single endangerment finding has since been used by EPA to launch an unparalleled regulation onslaught.

The president has clearly used the CAA as a vehicle for the new regulations, which impose a tax in the form of carbon emissions to businesses to regulate proof of the ongoing attempt of the White House to ram through another method to increase the taxation of American Industry and those that depend on it.

But on the bright side, more than 60 Senators voted in favor of four amendments that to one degree or another, would restrain the EPA's power to regulate carbon emissions from farmers, manufacturers, and power plants. According to Senator Mitch McConnell (R-KY) "We the Senate will continue to fight for legislation that will give the certainty that no unelected bureaucrat at the EPA is going to make efforts to create jobs even more difficult than this administration already has."

The Copenhagen Money Grab

Today in Copenhagen, Denmark, Politicized scientists are joining the politicians who funded them to commence 12 days of deceptive global warming propaganda designed to trash capitalism and to promote more regulation, higher taxes, global governance, and global redistribution of wealth.

Anyone who believes that this country can afford to contribute 10 billion dollars a year each, to countries such as Bangladesh, Indonesia, and a bevy of central African countries (for God knows what reason) is not gifted with a great deal of intelligence.

At time in this country in which we find ourselves facing 10% unemployment, the largest national deficient in our nations history, and possible double digit inflation, how on earth does this president think that we can afford to fund the global redistribution of wealth? In addition, given the current data scandal, there is now no overwhelming evidence that global warming actually exist in any meaning way.

The very same researchers caught secretly emailing one another about how they rigged global temperature records are among the most prominent scientist framing what has come out of the Intergovernmental Panel on Climate Change (IPCC) on which all the Copenhagen doomsday predictions are based. Given all this, the Copenhagen meeting should be cancelled, at least until a whole new set of uncontaminated and honest data can be compiled and evaluated, which could take 10 years or more.

These so called climate "scientist" emails reveal that they had been destroying or altering data when the measurements didn't support their point of view. As a result, absolutely nothing they say can be considered trustworthy. Everything they have published should be thrown out and new research should begin again with new researchers.

Former Vice President Al Gore, the driving force behind this bogus science, should be stripped of the nearly half billion dollars he has made through this global warming fraud and have it redistributed to his victims, the ones forced to pay higher fuel and energy bills and more for almost everything else they buy because of new climate policies and regulations.

Anyone who has paid any attention to the global warming issue knew long ago that we were being lied to when a prominent climate scientist urged colleagues to "offer up scary scenarios" and make public statements without mentioning the doubt and uncertainties they had about "global warming".

And we will continue to be lied to this week by other socialist politicians in Copenhagen, by scientists they bankroll, and by the liberal media that has told you little or nothing about the emails that suggest global warming is a manipulated pseudoscientific frau that should lead to the firing of every scientist ever vaguely involved in it.

By distorting science to create an ideological agenda, Mr. Gore has destroyed whatever authority and credibility that he possessed when scientists began their research. By that same logic, with global warming being used to promote bigger government and higher taxes, we should find the gumption to ask Mr. Gore straight on to explain how he has accumulated nearly a half billion in his personal bank account. Now that, my friends would be a very interesting conversation.

A Shady Mess

Ten days ago, 3/20/2009, Barrack Obama named Andrew Stern, the President of the Service Employees International Union (SEIU) to the newly created Deficient Reduction Commission. The commission is so new that there is very little known about it other than what its name indicates.

Can someone possibly explain to me just what makes Stern qualified to serve on such a commission? Given his education (Bachelors Degree in Urban Planning from the University of Pennsylvania and a certificate in whatever from the "Midwest Academy" – a school that trains leftist community organizers to infiltrate labor unions), serving on that commission will be a stretch of his budgeting ability.

As far as I can determine, Stern is no more qualified to serve on that commission (DRC) than the Manager of our local Safeway store. He is however, the personal Guru to our President. Given that Obama himself has absolutely zero business experience or any executive experience whatsoever, has never made a payroll or created a budget of any kind, has never failed to vote yea on any spending bill while in the Senate, he also appears not qualified to sit on that commission.

Then too, no one seems o be able to define just what that commission actually does. I don't seem to be able to find anything that describes exactly what the DRC has been asked to do or what the qualifications are for membership. Reducing the deficient seems fairly self explanatory, but we don't need a commission to do that. That is the job of our legislature and the president. Perhaps the president has lost faith in Congress, but surely not in himself, that would be beyond imagination.

It appears to me that Obama has simply found another plum to gift his favorite guy. After all, the 44 visits Stern made to the White House last year must have strengthened that extraordinary bond the two men have with each other. Lacking an appropriate board or commission that suits Mr. Stern, the president simply created one for him.

A couple of weeks ago, Stern declared that the SEIU has spent $165 million on the election of Barrack Obama, and in support of his programs…even more..,now" it's time the SEIU received something in return" he declared. This is a man confident of his position in the White House pecking order. Such talk has given the press an indication that Obama is in the pocket of the SEIU. I have a feeling however, being placed on an obscure commission that no one ever heard of, is not going to make Stern willing to call things even.

The behind closed doors deal made with the union in which the union was exempted from, taxes on 'Cadillac plans" was not offered to small businesses or anyone else not offering up huge amounts of money in return. It would appear that was a very nice gift to the SEIU even if Stern did not think it adequate. The entire shady mess that has been the "Healthcare Debate" has been a total disaster for the president. Buying off Senators and paying back unions has been handled so badly, it begs the question: Who are these people we have sent to Washington?

Kneel and Kiss The Ring......Wait A Minute

I, have at times, truly believed that there is something driving our current president that is not in the best interest of this country. I am not saying that Barrack Obama is anything but a patriotic American, but what I am saying is this president has had mucb less regard for his own country than he absolutely must have to be the inspirational leader we so need at this time.

Seven days after his inauguration speech, he delivered another speech, this one to the Muslim world reassuring them that "We are not your enemy". The seemingly urgent timing of that message was odd and actually disturbing. In reality, we are not at war with Islam. We have never been at war with the followers of Mohammed but, we are at war with a group of religious terrorists who happen to be Muslim.

Since his election, Obama has continued to characterize America as a very guilty nation. America, according to its president, is guilty of arrogance, greed, and just about every other sin under the sun, but none worse than insufficient respect for Islam. Could someone please explain this conduct to me? Could someone please tell me why our president deems it necessary to bow and kiss the ring of a Saudi King, but not show the same respect to the Queen of England? Actually, I don't think our presidents, regardless of who they are, should bow to anyone, including the Emperor of Japan.

I would say to this president that yes, we are at war with the enemies of this country regardless of who they are. And no, we do not have anymore of an obligation to kneel to the King of Saudi Arabia than we do to any other foreign ruler. This is the strongest, most generous, and fairest nation on this planet. It is a sham that our President doesn't seem to believe that. And to those who are killing Americans in Afghanistan and Iraq, I would say this---we ARE your enemy.

In the past, this president has shown much more enthusiasm to take on cable news than to attack terrorists in the Middle East. That is not an opinion folks, that is an absolute fact. I wrote in a previous column that Obama was not in a hurry to make a decision in regards to a troop increase in Afghanistan. That was a while back and now to the surprise of everyone, and to the chagrin of the far left, he has finally determined that more troops really are necessary.

On September 16,2001, President George Bush, while speaking to the White House reporters spoke these words, "People have declared war on America and they have made a terrible mistake…My administration has a job to do and we are going to do it". In Oslo, while accepting his Nobel Peace Prize, Barrack Obama astounded his audience and most of the world by giving an acceptance speech that stated clearly that you can't win a war using an extended version of the Peace Corps. He was precise, strong, and by adding 30,000 more troops to combat, appears intent on taking the Afghan war to a positive conclusion.

As a result of that speech and his failure to get the health bill that he and the far left were looking for, things were not looking very good for Mr. Obama, but---things are really looking up for his country.

At the end of it all, the president finishes his first year in office with his popularity in free fall, his party dispirited and divided, and almost certain punishment at the polls only 46 weeks away. Some House Democrats are already retiring, and donors would have to be out of their minds to give money to a Democratic candidate.

Democrats should go home and enjoy Christmas instead of playing Grinch to the seniors of America by passing this attack on Medicare. But they won't, because the president wants a "legacy law" even when it is built on the betrayal of every Medicare beneficiary as well as future generations burdened by the massive deficits built into Obamacare. Frankly, I am starting to feel just a little sorry for our rookie President. Well—not really.

Lloyd- A Chavez Wannabe

A few weeks ago, I mentioned an Obama appointee named Mark Lloyd. Mr. Lloyd is the diversity Czar at the Federal Communications Commission. Mr. Lloyd has quite an interesting background, to say the least. The presidents definition of diversity is quite unusual, it defines diversity as people who look different, but think precisely the same way... which is a little anathematic to diversity.

Lloyd makes no secret about his admiration for Hugo Chavez, the Venezuelan dictator. He appears to admire the methods used by Chavez such as shutting down news outlets that have disagreed with the dictators political agenda. He has praised Chavez and has explained the Chavez revolutions on camera. Now it is not clear whether or not Mr. Lloyd realized he was taped at the time, but he gave a detailed account of the two Chavez revolutions and why one failed and the other succeeded.

- In the first, he failed to take over the media properties, and so was thrown in prison. After he was released, he developed a new plan that absolutely included a takeover of the media. This was, in Lloyd's own words, "a very good revolution" and is the reason he is still in power today.
- Now in order to take over the media, you create very onerous taxes on private media.
- When the media companies, including newspapers, TV, and radio outlets are forced out of business because of these taxes, you take those stations and award them to people you define as minority interest groups.

We have today in the Federal Communication Commission a man who can make this happen in this country with a little help from the boss. I don't know about you folks, but this scares the daylights out of me. I just want to know why we have someone of this ilk working in the White House. Why on earth does this President surround himself with people like Lloyd and Van Jones (another Marxist)? Jones is gone, but Mr. Lloyd is very much there and busy, too.

This brings us to Carol Browner. Now this is not the first trip to the White House for Ms. Browner. Browner was the very radical Environmental Protection Agency director under Bill Clinton. This lady is just about as leftwing radical as they get. So much so, she has advised her staff not send emails because emails cannot be destroyed. Really? And why would she want to destroy them? This begs another question. Why does this woman belong to Socialist International, a group that believes in an international socialist society? "This woman really thinks she can control behavior through energy policy. It is a very dangerous precedent for the nation", says political author Scott Wheeler.

Could someone possibly explain why our President has selected these particular people to help him manage this nation. I need to know, do you know?

Muckraking and Other Things

The term muckraker started its life partially with the advent of "Yellow Journalism" in the Hearst newspapers of the early 20th century in San Francisco. Through the decades, the term has taken on a meaning of its own. In the Sunday issue of the Benicia Herald (9/27/09), Joe Conason again illustrates the classic description of the word.

The word "racist" has become one of the favorite words of modern day muckrakers such as Conason. Apparently, these days, left wing writers have taken this word to mean anyone not agreeing with Barrack Obama. It is a form of journalistic cheating indicative of talent deprived writers needing a crutch. Conason clearly falls into that category.

Calling Glen Beck and Rush Limbaugh racist is muckraking in its worst form. Even the president, who Conason appears to worship on high, refrains from lowering himself to use such ridiculous language tom describe either man. Conason, on the other hand, has no problem at all displaying his lack of talent and class.

His comments regarding Carol Moseley Braun (who happens to be one prime example of a racist) was a classic example of selective guilt. I could list Braun quotations that are so clearly racist they make Limbaugh appear as a choir boy. Braun appears to have permission to say anything without negative comment from the press. The fact that Conason mentioned her at all is a perfect illustration of lazy and bias journalism.

By mentioning the "many" white people working at the White House, Conason opened up a whole new question. What percentage of the West Wing staff really is white? Is that percentage higher or lower than that of the bush White House staff? Chances are the percentage is much lower. President Bush had a large number of minorities working on hi staff, but there is no doubt there are more there now. And that is the way it should be. The residing president has the right and the responsibility to name his own staff as he sees fit.

What Conason fails to tell us is that it is the white "Czars" and Cabinet Secretaries in the Obama administration that are (with a few exceptions) the most dangerous to this country. And trust me, Mr. Beck and Mr. Limbaugh know that well. There is no racism that can be attached to either of these men. Can the same be said about Mr. Conason? If this man is an example of the writing staff at the New York Observer, then my low opinion of the New York press is fully justified.

Declaration from the "Enemy Camp"

On December first, the president of this country gave a relatively short speech in which he announced a 30,000 troop increase in Afghanistan. Shortly thereafter, Chris Mathews of MSNBC declared that the President has made that speech from the "camp of the enemy". That so called "enemy camp" just happened to be the U.S. Military Academy at West Point.

Now... I understand that Mathews along with his partner Keith Olberman, represent a very radical wing of the Democratic Party, and he has been guilty of ridiculous and politically bias comments in the past. (Anyone remember the "tingles up the leg" comment during the campaign?) But this one has really disturbed me. Did he actually call West Point an "enemy camp"?

Yes, he did..and with enthusiasm...and he and the rest of the gang at MSNBC thought nothing of it. And to compound the nastiness of that comment, no one in the mainstream media has said a word about it. No one has commented about how such a small man has been given such a large platform to spew such ignorant and sickening commentary. Actually, the platform is miniscule in comparison to competition in that time slot from Fox News, but that is not of much importance compared to the obscene nature of the statement. There are those that will read this and ask themselves...why is this man making a fuss over what was a bad choice of words? But this choice of words was an example of the underlying bias saturating media commentary in America.

I am personally outraged by this obviously offensive and totally ignorant statement from a man whose intelligence has been completely overwhelmed by his arrogance and political bias. The location in which that speech was given was chosen by the President. It is obvious that he chose it in order to present the impression that he was a staunch military supporter. Whether or not he succeeded in doing that is not clear, but one thing is perfectly clear, Chris Mathews doesn't support out military.

There is an atmosphere of duplicity in this administration that defies reality. Lies are not lies and the truth is always doubtful. The extraordinary lack of experience across the board surpasses any previous administration, without a doubt. This president possesses an ego so ridiculously extravagant that it defies explanation. When one has spent life seldom ever hearing the word "no", the word doesn't register. The total lack of enthusiasm in Tuesday nights' speech signals little commitment and a look in the eye that indicates mild panic. Being able to please opposite factions with one set of facts is a result that even this man of the magnificent ego is not likely to achieve.

As for Mr. Mathews, well…unfortunately, the world is full of men and women who are credited with far more intelligence and moral backbone than they have ever possessed.

On a related note: In Obama World, politicians must always sound like politicians, they should never speak or act against type. His speeches are the equivalent of the Lifetime Channel, pretentious and full of drama. There appears to be some of "holiness" attached to his unadulterated strain of pure fantasy, and it permeates this administration.

The truth appears to this president as he deems it to be. Facts are what fit the occasion at the time. The president has a flair for making past events fit his agenda. He has a method of fact re-construction that would be amazing to observe if it were not so alarming. It is time for this president to stop viewing himself as a Shakespearian actor and to listen to his field generals over Washington politicos, just as he did in February of this year when approved the initial 21,000 troop increase and stated, "the world cannot afford the price that will come due if Afghanistan slides back into chaos". Amen!

The Crime of Mendacity

Since early January of this year, this country has surged toward an unclear destination. What we have always assumed our future to be, is now… not so certain. We have been running headlong toward a future full of uncertainty and we don't seem to realize it at all. The most startling aspect of this situation is our failure to recognize outright lies.

From the very beginning if his presidential campaign Mr, Obama has pretty much told it "like it is". He has done this over and over again and no one seems to have noticed. And…now that the press is beginning to come out of its coma, we are starting to notice that we aren't too sure we like it.

There have been political writers from the beginning that have put forward the theory that this president was the "chosen one" of a certain group of power brokers set on taking back the White House by any means possible. Without a doubt, this was the perfect man for that endeavor.

Barrack Obama is bright, articulate, superbly educated African American with little or no paper trail to drag him down. How could there be more perfect candidate to excite America at a time when this country was fed up totally with George Bush and everything happening in America.

The time and the circumstances surrounding this candidate were perfect, but it all depended on total control of the mainstream media. Given a blind press, this young man could pull off the feat of having absolutely no experience in addition to making promises time and again on which he knew he could not make good. The press simply looked the other way and here we are nearly a year into his Presidency and he has accomplished absolutely nothing. He and his party have tripled the national debt, the wars in the Middle East go on and on, and we are about to be saddled with some of the most horrendous Congressional bills in the history for this country. And the President's comments on all of this: "I inherited this all from George Bush!" And the most frequent, "Well I told you what I was going to do!" Well…you know what..he did tell us what he was going to do. He told us over and over and time and time again!

"I am going to change the culture of this nation as you know it" he told us early and often. And he is doing it, but how the press is noticing and the nation is starting to wake up to the fact that the "chosen one" is not the messiah he was made out to be.

The near panic aspect of his campaigns to pass ridiculous and dangerous bills in Congress is based on the knowledge that these have to be passed as quickly as possible or the whole thing could collapse. So now the panic lies begins. Now the handpicked team of radicals he keeps in the White House are going to have to earn their money. But don't worry, Obama will do his part. Yesterday, he told the press that he never ordered his Attorney general to move the terrorist trial to New York. Can you say Mendacity?

As a side note: this administration appears to have a suicidal reluctance to name it enemy and pursue him wherever they find him. If the continue this behavior, we will remain very conspicuous target, not only on foreign soil, but right here at home. And, if the American Army cannot defend its own---again: its own---then how can they defend the rest of us. Some one should have a talk with General George Casey and explain to him that he is paid to be a military commander and not Chief of Washington, D.C. Political Correctness Corps.

An attack on Christian rights at Hastings

There is an extremely important legal matter going on at this time in the Bay Area that involves Hasting School of Law (a U.C. Berkeley Law School), the Hastings Christian Legal Society, and the Supreme Court. And it is a very serious matter that the national media has made nearly invisible.

This case has it share of absurdity, but what is missing is obvious outrage. It is about the school denying recognition to the Christian Legal Society campus chapter because it will not have atheists or homosexual as officers. This is patently absurd on its face. This is like the Ethical Treatment of Animals Society- aka PETA- being forced to make the CEO of Hormel Meat Corporation their chairman of the board!

The man who would be dictator

I have begun recently to look into the expulsion from Honduras of President Manuel Zelaya. It would appear, looking at the facts behind the expulsion, that the Congress in Honduras felt that Zelaya was moving forward a constitutional referendum that would have allowed him to continue as president past one term. Given that Zelaya was widely known for his intense admiration for Hugo Chavez, the dictator in Venezuela, the move was not especially shocking.

What is more hocking is the reaction of the American State Department headed up by Hillary Clinton. With the approval of Clinton, the Organization of American States (OAS) suspended Honduras. The last country suspended from the organization was Castro's Cuba, forty years ago. Zelaya immediately warned the new leader Roberto Micheletti that the International Community has turned against him.

Could someone please explain to me what is going on here? As far as I can determine, Zelaya was expelled from the country by the duly elected and totally legal Congress of Honduras. The move came days after Zelaya fired the armed forces chief, who had refused to back the referendum plan. The Honduras constitution forbids the extension of a non-renewable four year term.

It appears to me that the action of the leader of the Congress in Honduras (Micheletti) was well within his constitutional right as leader. What I stunning are the actions by Clinton to subvert the perfectly legal right of the government of Honduras to handle these seditious actions by its president.

This brings us back to the stand taken by Clinton in support of a man who clearly would be the dictator of Honduras had the congress of that nation not taken action. Where exactly did that American support really come from? Any guesses? I have one. Where does all of our international policy decision originate? It comes from the man in the Oval Office. And why would Obama support this man who would be dictator so openly? Well... Hillary Clinton won't say, she is just loving this.

What I do know is this president has, for a very long time, chosen some very suspicious playmates. From Rev, Wright to bill Ayers, to the Rathke brothers and their creations ACORN and SEIU which are without question socialist experiments in this country. And he supports these people because he can. It is simple folks! He can and he does and he doesn't care what you think about it. In the case of Mr. Zalaya, it is just another example of the Obama plan for this country. Why is no one talking about Honduras? Where is the media when we need them?

Thou shall not pass this bill

Three thousand, four hundred and twenty five. 3,425. That is the number of times the word "shall" appears within those one thousand nine hundred and ninety pages of the Pelosi Congressional Health Bill. You know, the one she proudly passed this past week end. Given that this word appears only 306 times in our entire Constitution, it would appear that Nancy and company really wanted us to know that they mean business.

Of course, many of the shalls in our Constitution refer to liberties that the government shall NOT abridge, such as freedom of speech, press, religion, and assembly. But the shall in the Pelosi-Care bill appear to refer to freedom we once had, but shall not have in the near future if this bill his its way. This bill, according to noted Conservatives in Congress, "the biggest snatch of liberty in our nation's history, American liberties are under siege".

I have to tell you folks, the Pelosi legislation has absolutely nothing to do with making health care affordable or available. It is a government power-trip. It takes just one foot in the door and then...well you know the rest. Our founding fathers never intended the central government of this country to have any power not expressly set down in the Constitution. This Constitution refers to a federal government that shall do relatively little while the states, local communities, and individuals shall do what they wish, as long as they don't interfere with the personal and property rights of others.

There are sections of this bill that provide for hefty fines (up to $5,000) for failure to purchase insurance, and even jail time if that is not incentive enough to make one do the "right thing". That is in the Bill. Should you not take my word for it, I suggest you read it for yourself. Somewhere in that mass of 1,990 pages, it's in there. And that is how these obscene bills get passed, no one wants to read the things. They have been doing it this way for ages. And it stinks.

Are you aware that this Pelosi bill, the one she is so darn proud of, passed by only 2 votes in the House? Were you aware that 39 Democrats voted NO? This atrocious thing was so obscene it has been called the worst piece of legislation ever presented to Congress. And why for God's sake is this happening? Given the number of uninsured that will actually be affected by this legislation, the cost can not possibly be justified. In addition, it will still leave over 10 million people without health insurance, and another five million that might go to jail if they fail to buy a policy the government say they can afford.

Over the years, nearly every president has sought some form of Health Care legislation. It seems that this is the political "Holy Grail" for these people. But this President wants much more than insurance for the poor. What he wants is something akin to the European version of Social Medicine, a system that has proven, without a doubt, to be a disaster in nearly every country in which it has been introduced.

If we are really lucky, the Senate will see where all this is going and dump it in the toilet where it belongs. But don't get too excited, these are persistent people in the White House and this administration is just 10 months old and a trillion today is a billion of 2 years ago.....isn't it? God help us.

Can Anyone Say P.C.?

Has anyone noticed that over the years, Senior Military Officers have become more political than warriors? A week after a Muslim jihadi gunned down more than forty men and women at Fort Hood, Texas, one of this countries top Generals was still unwilling to admit that the attack had come from a Muslim. The fact is the November 5th attack was not just of terrorism: it was an act of war. And the actions of George Casey are an act of political correctness. Both are a tragedy and inexcusable.

By failing to acknowledge the fact that connection, this administration, with the constitutional duty to defend this nation "against all enemies foreign and domestic", has substituted a policy correctness at the expense of military readiness.

The fact is, there had been a concentrated effort from the beginning to keep Major Nidal Hasan's nationality and religion a non-issue. But his yelling "Allahu Akbar" while shooting unarmed military personnel, was a clear indication, don't you think?

For some strange reason, it has been critically important to this President that military personnel with a Muslim religious background be protected from bias in all branches of the service.

But really folks, this man had not been hard to identify as a religious jihadist. There is no reason this murderous assault at Fort Hood should have occurred. His motives and intentions were expressed loudly and clearly as far back as 5 years ago. But just as declarations of war by Al-Qaeda and the Muslim Brotherhood, they have been willfully ignored. Shouldn't the Commander in Chief of the U.S. Military have known about that man? If not, how about General Casey? If not Casey, how about Hasan's commanding officer? For God's sake! Someone should have had the gumption to report this man. Wait….. that's right! Someone did.

Actually several did and no one sounded the alarm. Can you say Political Correctness?

This administration appears to have a suicidal reluctance to name its enemy and pursue him wherever they find him. If they continue this behavior, we will remain a very conspicuous target, not only on foreign soil, but right here at home. And if the American Army cannot defend its own- against its own- the n how can it defend the rest of us? Someone should have a talk with George Casey and explain to him that he is paid to be a military commander and not chief of the Washington Political Correctness Corps. Anyone want to volunteer?

This week, a 23 year old Nigerian man, the son of a wealthy banker, failed at igniting a bomb while on a commercial flight over Michigan. After 3 days of silence. The president gave a 6 minute report in which he stated that the man was "isolated extremist" and not connected to any terrorist organization. What can I say? Here we go again.

The Oval Office-------A Union Hall?

In the year 2009- the first year of the Obama Administration, Andy Stern, then President of the SEIU labor union visited the oval office 44 times. You remember Mr. Stern don't you? He is the Andy Stern that the President spoke of in a taped speech to the convention of the union in which he said" when I need to talk to someone in regard to the problem of working men and women of this country-- I go to Andy Stern!

During this speech to the union membership, Obama repeated tht sme mantra 12 times. He did it with the emotion of a gospel tent preacher. He was riverting and obviousl;y full of devoted fervor. "I am not a newcomer to this, I have spent my adult life working on behalf of this union" he barked. In the spirit of that devotion, the President recently nominated radical labor lawyer Craig Becker to the National Labor Relations Board (NLRB). Now Becker is not only a very radical labor attorney, he is also the top lawyer at the Service Employees International Union (SEIU).

While working for the SEIU, Becker helped write three pro-labor executive orders that Obama signed just a week after taking office. The effect of the Stern influence on this President had already begun. An important milestone was reached last year when, for the first time, the majority of union members (51.4 percent) were state or federal government employees. The political power of government workers unions is a major reason why government spending is now out of control. And an undeniable reason the State of California is nearly bankrupt at this time.

The average pay for federal workers in Washington is now $94,047, whereas the average pay in the private sector (providing you are working) is $50,028. Annual raises are a matter of course, and government employees enjoy close to lifetime job security and benefits that include retirement. In the last 18 months the number of federal employees making $150,000 has doubled.

Another Washington lawyer, Joe Sandler, who is described as a "renowned expert on election law", has created a voracious gathering of front groups whose goal is to undermine the Tea Party movement. This bunch has funneled vast amounts of union dues money, including $10 million from the American Federation of State, County, and Municipal Employees (AFSCME) into fronts with innocuous names such as "Patriot Majority" and "Citizen for Progress". To defeat proposition 8, the SEIU spent $500,000 and the California Teachers Union spent $1,250,000. After the voters approved the measure, over 50 unions (including the AFL-CIO) signed a brief asking the courts to overturn the will of the people.

Recently, the Senate (in a rare show of common sense responsibility) rejected Craig Becker and Tom Harden and introduced a measure to abolish the Senate filibuster. Good luck on that on, Senator, given that it would require 67 votes which old Harry Reid can not possibly muster.

The prospective nominees who are reputed to be on Obama's short list for the next Supreme Court vacancy are weirdos of various flavors. One says it's OK for the Indiana Legislature to open with an invocation to Allah but not Jesus. Another calls himself a transnationalist and wants to integrate foreign law into the U.S. domestic law. Another wants dogs to have lawyers and says the government owns the organs in the body of any person who may die soon, and can remove them without consent. I am not making this up folks! God help us!

The state is in unbelievable turmoil. The single greatest cause for this, is out of control government unions (SEIU). There was a time in this country when labor unions were the salvation for the working man. Because of unions, pressure was brought on tyrannical corporations and American manufacturing to the point that the working man was afforded fair treatment and pay. That is no longer true and has not been for a very long time. If the truth were told, the blame for the near destruction of the American auto industry would be placed where it belongs on the auto unions. It is hard to say where all this is taking us as individuals, but none of it will ever change as long as this state continues as a one party enterprise.

Net Neutrality. "What"?

On October 13, 2009, I sent a piece to the Herald for consideration that spoke to the "Mark Lloyd" virus currently infecting the West Wing of the White House. Mr. Lloyd, who is a self described Marxist /Communist, currently functions as the Diversity Czar at the Federal Communication Commission. That is right, the same FCC that as I write, is trying to take control of the Internet, the World Wide Webb.

Mr. Lloyd, who has a very strong admiration for Hugo Chavez, has wasted no time in taking the Commission toward a government takeover of the Internet that will stifle innovation and further depress the job market in this country. Lloyd has made no secret of his intention to include wireless broadband in these rules. But, recently, Sen. John McCain has introduced the Internet Freedom Act of 2009 that would keep the Internet free from those government controls and regulations.

It has been no secret that Obama has placed in his West Wing, a group as remotes from that intention as one could ever imagine. Mark Lloyd has been given the job of doing whatever is necessary to formalize a set of net neutrality principles in place since 2005. McCain has called those proposed rules a "government takeover of the internet". Such a move on the part of the President is unprecedented and simply cannot be allowed to happen.

It is hard to tell if McCain can get the bill passed due to the majority of Democrats in both houses of Congress who support the net neutrality rule. But recently, a large number of House Democrats have made their concerns about the bill clear to the FCC. In a previous column, I described the methods used by Hugo Chavez to shut down free thought in Venezuela. This "Chavez" man at the FCC, Mark Lloyd, has studied his idol well and an actual move toward that end in this country is not with possibility.

Barrack Obama cannot be unaware of the actions of this surrogate. Given the opportunity, Lloyd could introduce rules and regulations that will give the government "de facto" control of wireless broadband in this country. Is it possible that Lloyd could do these things on his own? I think not. Actually, be can do nothing without the prior permission of the president. Which begs the question- who put Mark Lloyd in the West Wing? or for that matter, Carol Browner or Van Jones or Patrick Gaspard or Kevin Jennings? I think you get it. I truly hope you do.

What I am trying to say here does not pertain to the "Chicago Mafia", who act as buffers for Obama in the White House. The really scary people are in the West Wing and they are totally dedicated towards changing our government and our society to one that more resembles that of Socialist Europe. And folks, they are in a HURRY!! This president wants it now, socialized medicine is just the opening salvo. When Obamas' backers were chanting CHANGE, during the election last year, did they have any idea just how serious this man was? Well…you are going to see, and quickly. "Whether you like it or not".

What did you say Mr. Robinson?

A few days ago, I received from my lovely daughter Pamella, a column taken from the Gig Harbor, Washington newspaper. Pamella is a long time resident of that beautiful little town. The article written by Washington Post columnist Eugene Robinson, gave me cause to stop and think about what is happening to journalism in this country.

This article, in essence, was a sharp rebuke of any criticism of Barrack Obama being awarded the Nobel Peace prize. Now this column, when compared to some others in the press, was comparatively mild mannered, but, his reasoning was not up to par with his past excellence in writing. It was like watching someone trying to force an orange down the neck of a coke bottle. It just didn't fit. The whole piece was a "stretch" and not something of which Mr. Robinson should be particularly proud.

I have followed Eugene Robinson for many years and have rated him among, if not the best, political writer of the Post. His attempt to find some logical reason to give the president this award, however, was a total bust and failed to convince me, and I would assume any other commonsensical individual, that there was a reason for the award other than pure politics.

Now this is not the first time that this particular prize has gone to an individual with less than perfect credentials. Several characters come to mind, Asser Arafat being the first. But, this man, during the period of eligibility, which ended just two weeks into his presidency, had done nothing that would lead anyone to believe that he deserved a Nobel Peace Prize.

Trying to force that orange down that coke bottle neck has never been harder, has it Mr. Robinson? Castigating someone who recognizes how hard it is to justify that award is the act of a small person and I just don't see Eugene Robinson being a small man. Nevertheless, he has equivocated flowery speeches and great ambitions with real results. Simply put, wise men do not give the most prestigious award on this planet to someone who has high goals, glorious visions, but absolutely nothing to show for it at this time.

Perhaps before his term ends in 2012, Mr. Obama just might earn that award. No one would like to see that happen more than me, but until that does happen, the Nobel Prize has lost a great deal of its glitter. Mr. Robinson's column was full of "what ifs", what if the President does this or what if he accomplished this? Will people believe him deserving then? Well, they probably will., but he already has the prize. So just what did he do during the eligibility period to earn it? That bottle neck is not getting any wider. Mr. Robinson.

Safety Is Our Priority

In order to understand the meaning of victory, you must first define your enemies...and your allies. President Obama, in regard to Afghanistan, clearly does not understand the nature of the Jihad, and the devastating power of religious thought.

Thoughts can become weapons, philosophies are distinct reasons for war and good intentions are the most destructive of all. A belief extended by aggression can become the most dangerous of weapons. Some societies thrive on warfare, take that element away, and these nations stagnate. The flesh may not be excused from the laws of matter, but the mind is not so fettered. Thoughts transcend the physics of the brain, and this man, this president, possesses an ego so extraordinarily large that it has overtaken his common sense. He can be wrong, he is often wrong, but he refuses to even consider such a possibility. Never in the history of this nation have we elected a president so enthralled by his own intellect.

The American people are slowly coming to the conclusion that there is something in this man's background, in his core beliefs, that emboldens him to such a degrees that he is convinced that his superiority places him above error. This leads to his refusal to see the devastating power of the Muslim religion when given to radical groups such as the Taliban in Afghanistan.

Perhaps it is his early Muslim education in Indonesia that has shaped his understanding of the religion. Seldom are children taught the dark side of any religion, particularly in Muslim schools in Jakarta. Anyone who has studied the Muslim religion in depth is aware that it has been, throughout history, continuously exported through war and violence. Not to say that the religion itself is one of violence, but the exportation certainly has been bloody for nearly one thousand years.

Before the howls start (from a certain percentage of reading this), yes… the Christian religion is guilty, very guilty of some of the same aggression. But it ended centuries ago. What we have now in the Middle East, is full blown Jihad. Believe it, folks, it is for real and it is aimed at this country. Any failure to recognize it for what it is, can and will lead to another attack on America from Muslim radicals. This president, and an alarming number of like minded politicians, apparently refuse to see it coming. This cannot be tolerated. Something must be done about it before is too late.

Given the fact that George W. Bush prevented another attack for 8 years, it would be reasonable to assume that our current president, (for obvious reasons) must make the safety of this country his top priority. But I am sorry, folks, I just don't see that being as important to this man as a possible Nobel Peace Prize for which he is currently being touted. Now that is scary, so very scary.

The EPA Power Grab

The last time I checked, the EPA was a governmental organization tasked with the job of protecting us folks from big corporate polluters and environment crooks. No one at the EPA was elected to their job or vetted any way in regard to their personal opinions of environmental causes.

Unfortunately, this organization has recently morphed into a political entity more interested in satisfying left wing environmentalist than doing the job it was designed to do. Under the Obama administration, these people have been given the authority and permission to regulate nearly everything in this carbon based economy.

Politically, it is pure genius, engaging at once every left wing erogenous zone: rich mans guilt, post colonial guilt, and environmental guilt. But the idea of shaking down the industrial democracies in the name of the environment thrives not just in the refined internationalist precincts of Copenhagen, it thrives on the national scale too.

The EPA's ruling that it is authorized under the Clean Air Act to regulate emissions of carbon dioxide, is based on a "technical support document" or TSD. This TSD therefore, relies most heavily on the major assessment reports of the intergovernmental Panel on Climate Change (IPCC). Conservative think tanks are calling for the Obama administration to revoke its declaration that carbon dioxide is a dangerous pollutant subject to EPA regulations on the grounds that the primary source of information for the finding was the intergovernmental Panel on Climate Change. In essence of all this is an EPA attempt to force Congress to pass Cap and Trade by declaring "if you don't it,--------it will be Cap and No Trade!

It is this IPCC document the EPA used to support its preliminary finding, which in turn provided the underpinning for the endangerment finding issued on 12/07/2009. In other words, the findings were based on junk science. News that the EPA admittedly relied "most heavily" on robust and valuable "information from an organization that is caught up in climate gate triggered calls for the administration to withdraw the endangerment finding altogether.

The EPA rulings could be tied up in court for years, but voters have good reason to be worried over this administration's intentions. Watch out for the heavy breathers! The EPA says the very breath you are emitting is dangerous to others' health! They are kidding---aren't they folks?

Post note: Today the conference on climate control ended in Copenhagen. To say that little was accomplished is a gross understatement. Mr. Obama came to the party and left with nothing. Given that he gave the conference only two days of his time, he surely could not have expected any other result, but folks, you can bet your life he did, and leaving like a whipped dog was not part of his plan. Yet, that was not a B+ performance even by his grading system, and the result was predictable.

The president, however, actually believed he could fly into Copenhagen, dazzle the masses assembled, and walk away with a signed plan to save the world from a great flood, and the rain forest of South America all in the same day. In addition, convince China and India to give all the countries of the third world 30 billion dollars a year each for the next ten years and have them thank him for the privilege. Reality is a stranger to this man.

Now if you can hire a first rate law firm to bring a class action law suit against Albert Gore to retrieve that half a billion dollars he has stolen from the public, then things would be well with the world again.

2010
The Second Year of Obama

On Veterans Day 2010, instead of extolling America and our armed services, President Obama was in Indonesia celebrating its "Heroes Day", extolling its veterans who had sacrificed on behalf of their country and criticizing Americans for distrusting Islam. This man's habit of attacking his own country in front of foreign nationals was just beginning to hit is stride.

As early as 2010, Barack Obama had started to show this nation (in both word and deed) that he rejected America's founding ideals, which is why he promised to "fundamentally change this country", and why he had embarked on a disturbing course to fulfill his promise. America's greatness, for Obama, is not found in our freedom, tradition, or our protection of private property, rugged individualism, or equal opportunity. Instead, (to him) it depended on a hyperactive, benevolent government to stimulate the economy. Also, it meant initiating and controlling business activity and striving toward equality of outcome rather than of opportunity.

By this time, the Obama Presidency had already seen its share of bad economic news. While immodestly taking credit for the occasional positive development, Obama tended to deflect negative economic news by blaming American business or the American people themselves. The president's impulse to disparage America is intrinsic to his hard left worldview and adolescent education which led to those views.

The following political columns that I wrote during 2010 and that were published by the Benicia Herald and the Vallejo Times Herald, are indicative of what was going on politically at the time. Let me make it clear that the political atmosphere in Northern California tended to be more than a little bit left leaning and still does. Although these readers continued for the most part to be clearly "Progressive", they are absolutely all American and do support a strong America. I am proud to be a resident of Northern California and especially of Benicia and its neighboring towns. I hope you enjoy a look at what was happening at the time politically in Northern California and the nation in "2010" through the eyes of this newspaper columnist.

2010 Titles

The Second Year of Obama

Our European President

Once a Politician Always a Politician

Can You Explain Obama?

Where is The "Eco-Prophet" When You Need Him?

Political Cultures of Failure

Honduras Update

Where is the Love?

The Cloward-Piven Strategy

The Trial of Khalid Sheikli Mohammed

Why is Stern Leaving?

A Transparent Presidency—Really?

Some Very Greedy People

Social Democracy Doesn't Work

Where Do We Go From Here?

Very Scary Business

Al Qaeda and the ACLY

A Blatant Attempt to Socialize America

Afghanistan—It is Time to Leave

Answers from the Street

Climate Gate—It is not over

The White House- Union Shop

Situational Ethics

The Great Copenhagen Illumination

Somali Refugees

Sometimes the Truth is Painful

The press and the truth

The EPA Power Grab

The Law and the Left

Our European President

Almost immediately after his election, Barack Obama made a trip to Europe that he had promised himself he would make if ever elected president. During that trip the president daily confronted what he felt was the weaknesses and the blaring faults of his own country. It was like he just couldn't wait to get to his "favorite place on earth" and explain how he was going to make everything alright in a part of the world that is bleeding profusely from its own ineptitude.

There has never been a doubt that Barack Obama has a special place in his heart and mind for European Socialism. Starting with the initial trip, he has tried diligently to convince the leaders of the largest European economies that the way out of their financial problems was to spend MORE money.

Once A Politican Always a Politician

In Obama world, politicians must always sound like politicians, they should never speak or act against type. His speeches are the equivalent of the lifetime channel pretentious and full of drama. The idea that someone in the White House, for some mysterious reason, refused to fall on their sword, (behavior against type) seems to really bother the president. There appears to be some form of "holiness" attached to this unadulterated strain of pure fantasy that permeates this administration

The truth appears to this president as he deems it to be. Facts are what fit the occasion at the time. The president has a flair for making past events fit his own agenda. He has a method of fact reconstruction that would be amazing to observe, if it were not so alarming. His recent denial of any knowledge regarding huge government payments to the ACORN organization was extremely embarrassing, to say the least.

There was a report (on the internet) a few days after the ACORN statement that the president had ordered a staff member fired for not informing him that ACORN was receiving large government contracts. What on earth is going on here? Are we to actually believe that Obama was not aware that this organization (which he once represented in legal matters) was receiving those very lucrative contracts? If this report is true, then there is something seriously wrong with this mans mental processes or he told a blatant lie to his interviewer. Either way folks, we have a problem with this president. This is scary stuff.

Can You Explain Obama? 1/3/2010

Here at the beginning of a new decade, the prospects of peace and prosperity in America appear slim at best. I don't say that without a certain amount of trepidation and sadness, but I can't, for the life of me, get enthused about what appears to lie ahead.

As much as I would like to see him do so, our President appears incapable of understanding the complexities of this rather evil world we find ourselves living in these days. Given the narcissistic nature if the man, it is not altogether difficult to believe that he certainly believes that he does, but the evidence does not appear to support him.

As much as he would like to believe otherwise, radical Muslim organizations such as al-quida are hell bent on destroying our country and our way of life. We simply cannot afford to have a man in the White House who chooses not be believe and /or understand that.. Mr. Obama has done everything possible during this first year of his Presidency to turn a blind eye to what these organizations are planning.

His refusal to investigate the tragedy at Fort Hood and his immediate denial of al-quida involvement in the Detroit attack are just the most current and obvious indications of his reluctance to accept this evil for what it is.

I have come to the conclusion that this man simply does not want to see what is clearly in front of him, what is obvious to any other intelligent citizen in this country not currently employed in the West Wing of the White House. If this President continues down this road and the country is able to survive the next 3 years, he will not be re-elected. That is a fact.

Never before in the history of this country have we elected a President of which we know so little. Folks—we simply don't know who this man is or for what he stands for what he actually believes. If there are those of you reading this article today who feel you actually can defend and explain this man, would you please send a letter to the editor and give us you opinion? I would be so appreciative, and I don't think I would be alone.

Where Is The 'Eco-Prophet' When You Need Him?

Recently, I pursued a November 2009 issue of Newsweek magazine that contained a six page article on Al Gore. The article can only be described as an exercise in kneeling at the throne of an Environment God. Written by Sharon Begley, it could not possibly have been more positive in its description of Gore as the "Eco-Prophet" of our time.

Looking at this four month old article now only points up just how far Ms. Begley had trekked from the reality of February 2010. This piece, which used as its source a book by Gore titled, "Our Choice: A Plan to Solve the Climate Crisis", could today be refuted nearly totally. It's fascinating to read in retrospect.

In the article, Begley writes, "Despite suffering one of history's worst political fates, Gore has, by no means, given up on politicians". Reviewed nearly three months after the Copenhagen Conference, the writer's worship of Gore puts the spotlight on just how totally deceived the mainstream media, including political publications like Newsweek, were at that time. She also quotes Gore saying, "You know, the political system is (like climate), also nonlinear. I have been waiting a long time for that tipping point, when politicians and the people recognize the threat and act to avert it".

'But I think we are closer than ever," he continued. "Reality does have a way of knocking on the door". Yes it does, Mr. Gore. Yes it does.

Last fall politicians and the public recognized just how far Mr. Gore and his cadre of faux scientists had gone to convince the world of a phenomena that doesn't exist. Today reality is knocking on the door. But not the reality Albert Gore has preached to the faithful.

In two page article immediately following the Begley piece, Gore wrote, "I know that we waited too long. I wish we had acted sooner. But the outlook for the future is now bright. The wounds we inflicted on the atmosphere and the earth's ecological systems are healing.

"It seems ironic now that our commitment during the Great Transformation to a low carbon economy is what restored our economic prosperity. Once the world embarked on the journey to heal and save our future, tens of millions of new jobs- including whole new professions- have emerged.

Excuse me? The only person making money is Al Gore! Just where are all of these jobs? Where is all this restoration taking place?

O course, Gore wrote this before the Copenhagen Conference and shortly before the Anglia University emails were made public. Even given the fact that Mr. Gore was, at that time, supposedly unaware of the destructive nature of the emails, what he was saying was an example of unvarnished mendacity.

In the last few weeks, the hard core warming decriers has refused to recognize their failure to take responsibility for their false claims and now have described our current snow blizzards as the result of weather associated with the "climate change" phenomena. It now appears these people have determined that all forms of weather are the direct result of the humans breathing carbon into the atmosphere, The Environmental Protection Agency has gone so far as to declare it so and to create a huge tax machine to punish those having the temerity to "breathe".

And where is our champion Al Gore today? Perhaps he is up North looking for those polar bears he claims are becoming extinct.

All kidding- and snowstorms- aside, recent events have caused many to doubt the veracity of Gore's award-winning claims about man made global warming and the "settled science" behind climate change. The bottom line is that intelligent, responsible people are getting tired of being made to feel guilty for every carbon credit consumed and every gallon of gas burned, especially when it's becoming more and more clear that the current climate change hysteria is fueled less by scientific evidence than by an extreme ideology that-- much like Agent Smith in the Matrix movies-- views humanity as a virus.

Meanwhile, the number of people who would claim teat mankind has made zero impact on the environment in the past century is understandably small. Most reasonable, common sensical individuals—regardless of their party affiliation or their penchant for Birkenstocks and IMF protests-will agree there are many ways in which we can do better. Investing in renewable energy technologies, and modifying our personal habits to diminish our impact on the environment, and supporting efforts to achieve energy independence are all worthy and achievable goals. We are the "stewards"- mere caretakers- of creation, with the responsibility of managing the earth's resources not only for ourselves, but for future generations.

Al had the right idea, but the wrong motivation. The "green" Gore was thinking of was the color of money.

Political Cultures of Failure

In 1966 I attended a political meeting in the Wade Hampton Hotel in Columbia, South Carolina. It was a gathering of elected precinct officials in the state Republican Party and was held primarily to support Republican congressional candidates. The star of the show was former Vice President Richard Nixon. The room was full of sweat, cigar smoke and rage; the rhetoric; which was about patriotism and law and order, "burned the paint off the walls". As he left the hotel, Nixon is quoted as saying, "This is the future of this Party, right here in the South". He was correct by any standard.

Later, on the night of George W. Bush's second presidential election, the conservative movement seemed indomitable. In fact, it was rapidly falling apart. Conservatives knew how to win elections; however they turned out not to be very interested in governing. Throughout the decades since Nixon, conservatism has the essentially negative character of an insurgent movement.

Today, we have a relatively young man sitting in the Oval Office. He is all about speeches and campaigns and political cultures of failure. What he is not all about is governing this country. Perhaps he is on the level of 'THE ARCHITECT' Karl Rove when it comes to developing campaigns, but he appears to have little of no skill in running this country on a day to day basis. H e ran a political campaign in 2008 that will be written about for a long time into the future. It was chocked full of promises and predictions that were impossible to realize. The disturbing part of all this is: he was aware of that when he made them.

There are those out there that believe sincerely that this president made those predictions and promises simply to get elected. There are also those that believe he designed his campaign around his own "pie in the sky" fantasy belief that he could make these things happen. Whatever the truth is, this country is in a lot worse shape than it was when he was elected. This oil spill crisis is a sad indicator of his inability to "get the job done" and his consistent finger pointing and transference of responsibility when things go wrong.

This brings us to his seemingly difficult task of shifting gears after the campaign—from flying around the country, giving speeches that someone else has written—to focusing on the problems of state and the health of his country. It is perfectly clear at this time that Mr. Obama has not made that transition easily, if at all. Clearly the speeches and the constant flying are still with us——— and not likely to go away anytime soon——-if at all. Campaigning is primarily promises——-governing is seeing to it that those promises are fulfilled. The promises are the easy part of it. Besides, governing requires a conscience and quite a bit of skill.

Honduras Update

In a column a few weeks ago, I discussed the very odd behavior of the Hillary Clinton's State Department in regard to the expulsion from Hondurus of President Manuel Zelaga. Zelaya had been ousted by his own Supreme Court and booted out of the country by the army. For some totally unclear reason, Hillary has formed some sort of affection for the would be cowboy dictator.

Now thee is no argument in regard to the fact that Zelaga is a self professed Chavista, and would like very much to emulate his idol in Honduras, and no argument about the fact that Hillary Clinton, her State Department and her boss, Mr. Obama are very aware of it.

From the very beginning of this strange scenario, Clinton and Obama took a profoundly pro-Zelaya stance. Never mind the fact that Zelaga never has hidden his total affection for the Venezuelan Dictator Chavez. The government of Honduras acted in a perfectly legal manner in its actions to expel its president for sedition and his attempt to override the Constitution of Honduras in order to obtain an additional four years as president. Unfortunately for Mr. Zelaya, the same constitution forbids any term over four years.

The Zelaya answer to that was to fire the Commanding General of the Army who insisted onfollowing the constitution as it is written. The government answer to that was to arrest Zelaya, put him on an airplane and send him out of the country. Now it gets interesting.

Immediately following the ouster of Zelaya, Hillary Clinton demanded that Roberto Michelletti, the President of the Honduras Congress bring the president back and restore him to power. Michelletti refused and Zelaya later sneaked back into the country. And where is he residing? Well...the Brazilian Embassy. The same Brazil that is hosting President Mahhmound Ahmadinejad of Iran this week.

Is it me, or is there not something strange going on here? Just when did we start supporting would be dictators over a legally elected government that just happens to be a close friend of this country? And, if our president believes that his recent trip to the Pan-American Conference made him any new friends or strengthened our influence in the region, well...I have a bridge to sell you Mr. President.

The very fact that Iranian bad boy Ahmadineajad is in Brazil today is a clear indication that President Luiz da Silva has been influenced more by Chavez than by Obama. Extending such an invitation to the leader who hosted a conference of Holocaust skeptics and deniers, often predicts Israel will be destroyed, stole his last election and is stiffing the West on Iran's nuclear program, is clearly a poke in the eye of Barack Obama.

Where is the love?

After slightly over one year in office, the President of the United States has reversed its position on Israel, a position that has been in place for over 60 years. Israel is the only democracy in the Middle East and our only ally in the region. This president, who made a major speech in support of all Muslim faiths in Cairo, Egypt only weeks after his inauguration, has turned his back on Israel and badly insulted its Prime Minister within the last week.

In the past, presidents have been ill advised to reduce support for Israel. For no other reason than the reliable financial support American Jews have always given to the Democratic Party. In the last decade Pentecostals have joined American Jews in their support of Israel and the large majority of Christian Americans support the Jewish State. It has always been a given that this country would support Israel in their time of need.

But....folks, these are different times. There is a man in the White House today who feels no need or compulsion to continue that support. The horrific manner in which Prime Minister Benjamim Netanyahu was treated in his trip to Washington begs the question; what could possibly have given this president the idea that the American people could possibly condone that treatment? As a guest at the White House, Barack Obama left Netanyahu alone in a room without so much as a glass of water while Obama spent 2 hours upstairs having dinner with his family.

In a previous article, I spoke of the odd and disturbing timing of the Cairo speech, given that it came less than two weeks after Obama's inauguration. That speech indicated an almost desperate need to let the Muslim people around the world know that the days of total Jewish support was over and he was going to create a Muslim friendly administration. With this obscene display of insulting behavior, Obama has sent the message to Muslims around the world: You will now feel the love of this nation.

The studied humiliation of Netanyahu suggest a sinister agenda at work. By this behavior. There is no reason for Israel to catalyze peace negotiations when there is no, single entity that is both committed to peace and speaks for the entire Palestinian people. So Obama and Hillary Clinton have shown the Arab world that the United States is willing to throw Israel into the sea. When Clinton and Obama explode in indignation against Israel for building apartments in East Jerusalem, they deliberately miss the point. There is no reason for Israel to catalyze peace negotiations when there is no single entity that is both committed to peace and speaks for the entire Palestinian people. So why are the president and his Secretary of State so intent on raiding the profile of the construction issue and publicizing it? One suspects that an effort to link Israel resistance to the peace process to the ongoing loss of American lives in Iraq and Afghanistan, if not global terrorism of al quida.

Ultimately, the administration agenda may be to explain its withdrawal of support for Israel by blaming its stubborn insistence on housing construction. One can well see the Obama White House learning to live with an Iranian nuclear weapon while banning Israel for fomenting Iranian hostility by building housing.

All the while, through American aid to Gaza, the Obama administration is helping Hamas to solidify its position in Gaza and lengthen its lease on political power---the very power it is using to torpedo the peace process. This administration wants Netanyahu out. Specifically, they want him to feel such pressure that he dumps his rightwing coalition partners and forms a new government with left of center former Prime Minister Tzipi Livni, who thinks nothing of trading land for peace, no matter how flawed that peace might be.

Clinton is trying to use Obama's rejection of Netanyahu's course to force her way into the government. This administration's intent on helping her do so by publicly humiliating Netanyahu. Insanity is defined as doing the same thing over and over again and expecting a different outcome each time. Well—what can I say? I don't think Israel is feeling any love these days, but I doubt that our president is going to feel the wrath of Jewish Americans over the next 6 months.

The Cloward-Piven Strategy

How many of those reading this column today are familiar with Richard Cloward or France Fox Piven. These two were sociologists and political activists at Columbia University School of Social Work in the 60's who outlined a unique political strategy in The Nation Magazine. They argued that many Americans who were eligible for welfare were not receiving benefits, and that a welfare enrollment drive would create a political crisis that would force politicians "to enact legislation establishing a guaranteed national income".

Historian Robert E. Weir argues that the original goal of the strategy was to being about a crisis in the welfare system that would require radical reforms that were at their core methods of wiping out poverty by establishing a guaranteed income...(via) outright "redistribution of wealth". This strategy was designed to create a crisis in the welfare system by exploiting the gap between welfare law and practice, that would ultimately bring about it' s collapse and replace it with a system of guaranteed annual income. The authors of this strategy hoped to accomplish this end by informing the poor of their rights to welfare assistance, encouraging them to apply for benefits and, in effect, overloading an already overburdened bureaucracy.

There are a large number of latter day social reconstructionists, including our current president, who fell in love with this strategy as university students and continue to this day to advocate and encourage most of tits basic concepts. In fact, the West Wing of the White House is full of them. Van Jones, during the short period he was there, never stopped preaching at the Cloward-Piven pulpit. Our president has never denied that as a student, and still continues to this day to be a dedicated disciple of the church of "Monetary Justice".

All of the constant efforts of the Obama administration to Socialize this country are becoming very evident to anyone with an ounce of common sense and no Ivy League political career, consist primarily of community organizing and legal representation of entities such as Acorn, it should come as no surprise that he is predisposed to social activism. But he never said the "changes" he preached during his campaign for President included turning this country into a banana republic.

It has occurred to me that it is time that the people in this country start to examine carefully just exactly what our president is trying to do with this deluge of new bills in Congress. Is there a common thread tying all this legislation together? Is there an ultimate goal in all this hyper activity? I say there is and it has hardly been hidden out of sight. In fact, it is so out there "in plain sight", that it is nearly invisible to the average voter in this country. Now if all of that seems kind of creepy, well… it is! But what we are seeing is an all out assault on our traditional capitalist society. And I have to tell you folks, this president is wasting no time trying to make this assault successful. The urgency behind these bills begs a response by the American people. And that response should be, "No thank you, we want our country just as it is "!!

The Trial of Khalid Sheikh Mohammed

I graduated from a highly respected law school, even though it was a very longtime ago. And even though my knowledge of the a law was used primarily in my various businesses, I still retain quite a bit of the knowledge required to obtain that degree.

That said, I feel that I am qualified to make a few comments in regard to the upcoming trial of Khalid Sheikh Mohammed in New York. Simply put, the Executive Branch of our government is pre- determining what the judicial branch will and will not do. To those currently in the legal profession-where are you with all this? We are talking about an obvious "Show Trial" here that will be as much an indictment of the Bush administration as Khalid Sheikh Mohammed and the other terrorists who will be on trial there.

Recently, while being questioned in a Senate hearing, Attorney General Erick Holder was asked by Senator Lindsey Graham of South Carolina, if he had any knowledge of an enemy combatant ever being tried in a criminal court. After a few ahs and ohs, he was interrupted by Graham who said simply, "the answer is no, Mr. Holder".

The truth is these men are not criminals, they are enemy soldiers and prisoners of war. They are something the likes of which we have never seen before, and neither our law or even International law addresses how these men should be dealt with. But one thing is certain, they should not be tried in a civil court where they are given rights reserved for American citizens.

In the same Senate hearing previously mentioned, Holder stated that "failure is not an option" as if the outcome had been pre-determined. What has happened to "due process"? Is there some sort of "the fix is in" going on here? Could the prosecution possibly load the jury? Of course not, but absent that, how could Mr. Holder male such a confident statement to the Senate?

It is no secret that the outcomes of criminal trials are highly unpredictable. One has only to look at the O.J. Simpson and Robert Blake trials to know how true that is. And to compound all this, Holder's ability to answer Senator Graham's question appears to have done little to support his decision to move the trial to New York. How could Holder possibly be so certain of a conviction in a civil trial when KSM had already pled guilty in a military tribunal. Even in International law, pleading guilty is just that, and absent an insanity plea, no further process is required.

There is another question to be asked here. What would we do if KSM were found innocent, or any of the defendants, for that matter? To that question, Holder answered that "none will be released if found innocent"! Say what!... What is the reason for these trials, can someone answer that question for me?

The answer could be... that these trials are not so much trials of these terrorists, but more likely a trial of George Bush and Dick Cheney, big legal "show". Something to take our minds off all the failures of this administration to address even the simplest problems facing us at this time.

The idea of Barrack Obama and his Attorney General predetermining the outcome of civilian trials is a unsettling thing. Once again, I ask the American Bar Association, "where do you stand on this"? Holders' responses to Senate questions should be unacceptable by all Americans... even Democrat attorneys.

As added note: Monday night on the "CBS Evening News", Katie Couric stated that "Although President Obama has been in office less than a year, many Americans are growing disenchanted with his handling of the enormous problems he and the country are facing, from healthcare, to unemployment, to Afghanistan. His poll numbers are sliding, and at least one poll shows his job approval has fallen, for the first time, below 50%." The President is getting battered on everything from the economy to foreign policy. Some polls show Americans are increasingly questioning his credibility"

The CBS report also criticized the President for being "indecisive" on Afghanastan, and for returning from his recent Asian trip "with little to show for it". Also on the program, an expert described Obama's trip ", the "Amateur Hour" as he did not line up agreements with foreign countries before venturing abroad.

According to Couric, "is the honeymoon over?" And all of this from a darling of the liberal media? Will wonders ever cease to happen? What an amazing and terrible turn of events for the President! To quote the Rev. J. Wright, have the "chickens come home to roost?"

Why is Stern leaving?

On the 14th of April, on the 10th pages of the A section of the S.F. Chronicle, there appeared a small article announcing the retirement of Andrew Stern, the President of the Service employees International Union. The very same Andrew Stern who visited the White House 44 times last year. The same Mr. Stern who the president called his "very closest friend and advisor".

And we are left with the question: Why is Mr. Stern retiring? He is a young 59 year old with a professed "very high energy level" in obviously good health, who occupied an extremely powerful position and is the envy of every executive in the labor movement. I admit that I was shocked to read that announcement, but even more shocked to read it on the 10th page of A section of the Chronicle.

Mr. Stern is a controversial individual, disliked by a great many on the political right. He is also not thought of too highly by the powerful leaders, of the AFL-CIO and several other national labor unions. Just recently he led a labor group in the San Francisco hotel industry out of the AFL-CIO into a new union which he (Stern) had created. Needless to say, there was a hue and cry and shouts of "traitor" among the AFL-CIO regulators and great distain among labor nationwide.

Stern has never hidden his Socialist associations and actually has bragged that labor unions in the past have not been "Socialist enough". He stops short of defining himself as a "communist" but does not appear to be offended by that label. This move, in connection with the downfall of the ACORN organization (at least under that name) sends a strong message that something odd is going on in the Obama triumvirate which includes, along with the president, ACORN and Stern's SEIU.

The president's reluctance to investigate the antics of the SEIU is just short of illegal. I have mentioned previously that Stern is openly pushing the president for "a little payback". Stopping a legitimate investigation proceeding regarding union activities, whether they are legal, illegal or questionable is Obstruction of Justice. When someone with power seeks payment (this doesn't have to be monetary sum, it can be to change a final outcome of something) in exchange for certain actions or backing/support, that person is said to be peddling influence.

Regardless of who initiate the deal or threat, either party to an act of bribery can be found guilty of the crime independently of the other. Unions that throw their support to Democratic candidates and then threaten to pull that support in order to change the end result of an election or vote, are peddling influence. The unions did threaten Democrats, who would not vote in favor of the Healthcare Reform Bill, that they would pull funds and backing making it more difficult for them to be re-elected. Case in point, they threatened Joe Liberman and Bart Stupak that they would not support their efforts to be elected.

Stern's union was in favor of Obama/care when they themselves are exempt from being forced to take it, as was Congress, their families and staff members and their families, not to mention Muslims and the Amish. Well...it appears that Andy got a "little payback: in the health bill, but I am afraid "a little" is not what Mr. Stern was looking for, besides...the Federal Government cannot offer something to one group and discriminate against another. As a result, those aspects of the bill will be overturned by the Supreme Court.

Which still leaves us with the same question: why is Andy Stern retiring as President of the SEIU? Frankly, I don't know, but I am willing to bet you that the former entity known as ACORN will arise in a new form and with a new leader. Does anyone care to speculate as to who that might be? Ah, come on, you know!!!

In 1966 I attended a political meeting in the Wade Hampton Hotel in Columbia, South Carolina. It was a gathering of elected officials in the state Republican Party and was held primarily to support Republican congressional candidates. The star of the show was former Vice President Richard Nixon. The room was full of sweat, cigar smoke, and rage. The rhetoric which was about patriotism and law and order, "burned the paint off the walls". As he left the hotel, Nixon is quoted as saying, "This is the future of this Party, right here in the South". He was correct by any standard.

Thirty eight years later, on the night of George W. Bush's second presidential election, the conservative movement seemed indomitable. In fact, it was rapidly falling apart. Conservatives knew how to win elections: however, they turned out not to be very interested in governing. Throughout the decades since Nixon, conservatism has the essentially negative character of an insurgent movement.

Today, we have a relatively young man sitting in the Oval Office. He is all about speeches and campaigns and political cultures of failure. What he is not all about is governing this country. Perhaps he is on the level of "THE ARCHITECT" Karl Rove when it comes to developing campaigns, but he appears to have little or no skill in running this country on a day to day basis. He ran a political campaign in 2008 that will be written about for a longtime into the future. It was chocked full of promises and predictions that were impossible to realize. The disturbing part of all this is:: he was aware of that when he made them.

There are those out there that believe sincerely that this president made those predictions and promises simply to get elected. There are also those that believe he designed his campaign around his own "pie in the sky" fantasy belief that he could make these things happen. Whatever the truth is, this country is in a lot worse shape than it was when he was elected.

Jim Pugh

This oil spill crisis is a sad indicator of his inability to "get the job done" and his consistent finger pointing and transference of responsibility when things go wrong.

This brings us to his seemingly difficult task of shifting gears after the campaign—from flying frantically around the country giving speeches that someone else has written- to focusing on the problems of state and the health of this country. It is perfectly clear at this time that Mr. Obama has not made that transition easily, if at all, Clearly the speeches and the constant flying are still with us----and not likely to go away anytime soon---if at all. Campaigning is primarily promises---governing is seeing to it that those promises are fulfilled. The promises are the easy part of it. Besides, governing requires a conscience and quite a bit of skill.

Some Very Greedy People

For some reason there is one very important item being left completely out of the Obamacare Health Plan- Tort Reform. It appears that the president has asked everyone to sacrifice except the very group that is driving skyrocketing healthcare cost. And let's face it, this is a very special bunch of very greedy men and women who care not a dimes worth about the astronomical cost of that greed on the American people.

Why do you think lawyers have been exempted from any sacrifice at all? It is fairly simple, they have paid for that exemption. Paid for it with tens of millions of dollars a year contributed to Democrat candidates. Given that fact, no one could possibly blame the president if he looked out for the American Bar Association, could they? Besides…he happens to be, like most politicians, a lawyer himself.

Actually, there are millions of average Americans out there that don't like it a bit. The profession of law does not find its self in the highest of esteem these days. The cost of medical malpractice insurance has raised the cost of doing business to such an extreme that a very large number of doctors have actually left private practice.

Yet, this administration sees no conflict in ignoring this 700 pound gorilla in the Obamacare dining room. This big boy is planning on eating very well and no on seems to mind one bit. Well…there are those that mind, but they happen to watch Fox News and therefore are not to be considered seriously. There is a certain element in this country led by University elites that simply don't understand the mindset of the average guy who knows that there is something wrong about this President, even if they cannot explain their thoughts the way teachers can explain theirs.

I would suggest that this element not talk down to those with whom they obviously disagree. Education is a wonderful thing. I have a college degree myself, but this group evidently does not realize that more than one half of the people in this country do not agree with the educational elitist opinion of the president. I welcome this group of educators to look more closely at the people with whom this President surrounds himself. If they agree with these appointments, then we will know from where their political philosophy originates. Whatever that might be.

That brings us back to that big hungry gorilla at the Obamacare dining room table. Why has no one in the press (with the exception of those whacko rightwingers) asked the president straight on why he is totally ignoring the trial lawyers in this country in regard to what they are costing every single individual who has private insurance?

Perhaps someone could grace us with another article in which they explain just why it is perfectly correct for this President of "fluent brilliance" to do as he pleases. I look forward to that with great anticipation. As a side note, the huge majority of educators in this country lean solidly to the left. That should put whatever they support clearly in context. I truly hope so.

Social Democracy Doesn't Work

At the time I write this column there is one week left until we go to the polling place and elect a bevy of politicians and vote on numerous propositions that will no doubt alter the way we live today. By the time you read this the voting may be over and the deed will have been done. And will we do it right? That is hard to say, we can hope so.

This state and this country are in such bad shape that it staggers the imagination. The debt that both carry is unimaginable and yet we continue to elect people, both statewide and nationally, who spend money (yours and mine) like there is no end to the supply. Well…there is, folks. We are rapidly coming to the end of the supply line.

It won't be long before our government begins to print more money in order to pay its' bills. When it does, the value of your dollar will shrink in relation to the amount printed. And then…every single thing we buy will cost more, because the money we buy it with will be worth less. It is called inflation. It is death to an economy.

And yet we have a president and a congress who are wearing blinders. They refuse to see what is happening and how near we are to being a second or third rate nation. I am not talking about political parties here. Both of our most prominent parties are equally guilty of what has happened to this wonderful nation. And what part have we, as individuals, played in this debacle? Quite a bit I am afraid. This country no longer produces anything. And the less it produces, the more entitlements the people demand. Not jobs mind you, but entitlements.

For in this day and age, even the job is considered an entitlement. Jobs where you don't really have to work all that hard, but you surely have to be paid very well and given your health care and every other perk you could possibly desire. These days they are called government jobs. And…you see, since everyone wants government jobs, we don't need factories or any other private enterprise employment. This, my friends is called Socialism.

So…since we all want it, and everyone has these jobs, what is wrong with that? Well, let's see. First, there has never been in the history of this planet, a country that had a population over 20 million that ever succeeded in making Socialism work. Just look at the long list of nations that have failed. Starting with the biggest: Russia and China learned their lesson in the hardest way. Their people suffered in unimaginable ways for more than a half a century due to their Socialist/Communist system. A system they no longer have, and for good reason.

We have a commander in chief who is committed totally to a Democratic Socialist system of government. There are many of them around the world. The governments of Sweden and Norway and Holland are examples of this form of government. It has worked fairly well (up until recently) for these small countries, but folks, the larger the nation the more impossible it is for Socialism to prosper.

Recently even Sweden, which has had a cradle to grave system for half a century has begun to suffer greatly from cost which overwhelms the governments' ability to cover the outlay. It is a financial fact that the larger the country and economy, the harder it becomes to cover the cost. It simply does not work in nations as large as the United States. Surely someone as seemingly intelligent and educated as our current president should know that.

Well…obviously he does not or he simply doesn't care. And should you have forgotten, this is the same man who constantly denies he is a socialist, but insist on installing socialist programs. This is not an opinion, it is a fact. Take the time to check it out…you may just be shocked and hopefully enlightened enough to ask for a REAL change. Short of that, there is not hope for us. Now let the "progressives" of Benicia have their turn. This should be interesting.

Where Do We Go From Here?

With in the last few months, politics have gone sour on our president. According to the "Peter "Principle", if it can get worse, it will. And in regard to Barrack Obama, it has. The odd part of all this is the fact that this President does not seem or really care much if it does or not.

Recently, Obama has let it be known that he is not all that much concerned if he gets reelected or not. That is an astounding statement by a president that has been in office less than 2 years of his first term. According to Politico.com, the president has an agenda when first elected in 2008 and he feels that he has achieved a great deal of what proposed. Although a majority of the politically savvy would dare to differ.

It appears that the President goes in the polls, the more positive attention he is given by the mainstream media. It is as if he is a little boy given a pat on the head by a loving nanny. In his case it is a big, big hug and kiss. But lets face it folks, this president has failed at just about everything he has attempted to do in this first 2 years. The one huge bill he was able to force feed down the throats of the American people (Healthcare), is extremely unpopular and continues to act as an example of what our government can do…. regardless of the way the average American feels.

The total disregard for the well being of our citizens living on the Mexican-Arizona border, is beyond disgraceful and is just another example of the president burning another bridge. From a purely political standpoint, this president has little or no chance of carrying the State of Arizona in 2012 if he continues down this road of total abandonment of American citizens on that border. The attitude in the West Wing… "We didn't carry Arizona in2008, nothing to lose there".

The cynical say that it is all about the votes. Those ten million Hispanic votes that will surely go to Obama and the Democratic Party should be president's "Immigration Reform" go through Congress,. And really…

how can anyone with a clear head and half a brain, not see that his is the strategy that is in place in the Obama White House. Just look at what is going on all around us and it is hard to deny that there is not an agenda and it is wreaking havoc on the American people.

Big in the press this past week has been the Michelle Obama pleasure trip to Spain with the girls and several close friends. The cost of this trip to the American taxpayer …$1 Million Dollars. Even the President's Chief of Staff, David Axelrod, had a near heart attack when told of the trip. According to the Huffington Blog (yes, that Huffington Blog), there was quite a blow up in the Oval Office about that trip. Would it not be fair to say that this president and his wife are totally tone deaf when it comes to taking elite vacations in foreign countries and resorts of the rich and famous (Martha's Vineyard) in America while the resorts of the Gulf Coast are suffering a terrible disaster on their beautiful beaches?

On the East Coast, the press is full of news of a Muslim faction's attempt to build a Mosque on or near the site of the Twin Towers disaster. This, of course, has the approval of the president (no big surprise there). But what is surprising is the support of some big time New Yorkers like Michael Bloomberg, the Mayor, and Congressman Jerry Nadler (D-NY). As it regards Nadler, nothing is too surprising, but Bloomberg… I will have to admit…did catch me off guard. Not only did the president agree with the religious leader behind the group attempting to build the Mosque, he has actually named the same man to represent this country at a large Muslim gathering in the Middle East next month.

Excuse me? Could someone please explain the reasoning behind the move? I have to admit, when it comes to this President and his actions as they regard anything Muslim, I am at a total loss.

And that brings us back to the start of this article. It simply doesn't register with this man that most of the things he is doing as President simply do not cause positive reactions on behalf of the electorate. If he is playing "Chicken" with the American voter, then he is most likely a one term President. From his actions in the past, I would assume that was just what he expects. Go figure.

Al Qaeda and the ACLU

The news of recent attempts by the American Civil Liberties Union (ACLU) to end all drone aircraft attacks against Al Qaeda in Pakistan and other locations throughout the Middle East has finally reached the major media in this country. No small feat that. Al Qaeda, should you not be aware, is the terrorist organization headed up by Osama bin Laden, the same organization that planned and carried out the attacks of 9/11/2000 on the cities of New York and Washington.

The very idea that an American organization, made up of actual Americans, Americans of sane (?) mind, with American mothers and fathers, would actually defend and support these terrorists rather than the men of our military, staggers the imagination. The first inclination is to label these people as a bunch of crazies, albeit dangerous crazies, and a bunch that should have their passports lifted and shown the door, and for keeps. There is just no plausible explanation for this seditionist attempt to undermine our government---in some parts of the world—it would be called treason.

The American Civil Liberties Union has sued the Federal Government to learn the use of unmanned drones for targeted killings by the military, and the CIA. In particular, the lawsuit ask for information on when, where and against whom drone attacks can be authorized, the number and rate of civilian casualties and other basic information essential for assessing the wisdom and legality of using armed drones to conduct targeted killings. I must confess that I just don't understand the mind set of these people. But then, I don't have to understand this bunch to totally detest them all. The remarkable, part of all this is the free pass this group gets by the mainstream media in America. I have lobbed them all (the ACLU, the media, and the administration) together into one despicable brotherhood. This works very well for me. Somehow there is something totally NOT American about this group. Even the name of this organization is a misnomer.

The very strongest supporter of the ACLU in Washington (exempting the president) is the Attorney General of the United States, Eric Holder. He and his former New York City law firm, in conjunction with the ACLU, have defended over 30 of these Al Qaeda terrorists over the last ten years and several of these same lawyers are now working for the Justice Department headed by Holder. In the last year, Holder has attempted to move the terrorist trials from Cuba to New York City. This, to my mind, is indefensible, and Holder is a disgrace to the office, but no more guilty of gross miscalculations than his boss---who has given him the green light---and then withdrew his backing. At this point, we don't know where they will hold these trials, if they hold them at all.

The simply astounding actions of this leftist organization, particularly its recent lawsuit against the United States in regard to those drone attacks, leaves any intelligent, patriotic, American with no other choice than to insist on a complete investigation of the entire group. I cannot understand how George Miller or any other member of Congress could possibly decline to do so. This organization (ACLU) has the support of nearly every leftist group in the country (would you believe the American Communist Party?)---who themselves have the support of every leftist overlord in the country, such as George Soros and a bevy of Hollywood lightweights like Alec Baldwin and George Clooney whose combined intelligent quotient might reach 95.

The ACLU has long been one of the most controversial organizations in the country, and it has never been shy about its left-wing –Socialist bend. It has also never been shy about its support from some rather shady sources such as the American Communist Party. In addition, liberal lawyers, particularly graduates if prominent East Coast law school such as Columbia, Yale and Harvard, have long provided large amounts of monetary and moral support.

In return, the ACLU has supported and provided legal assistance to some of the most outrageous and controversial legal stands in the history of jurisprudence in this country. The ACLU has always looked down its nose at the "common" laws of America. Instead, it has specialized in supporting various groups and organizations that represent the dregs of all segments of our society. In addition, it has also preferred to represent clients who, for the most part, stood for clearly anti-American causes. In fact, it appears rather proud of that position.

The pending law suit against the United States by the ACLU, in regard to attacks on Al Qaeda bases and leaders, has no standing and simply no chance of prevailing at this time. Despite the huge number of proud leftist judges in America, this one will not succeed. Not now or ever. The parade of politically correct leftist causes will have to find another champion. And perhaps they should be looking for a first class attorney to represent their own organization. They just might be needing one.

According to Jameel Jaffer, Director of Policy of the ACLU National Security Project, "These kinds of questions ought to be discussed and debated publicly, not resolved behind closed doors. While the Obama administration may legitimately withhold intelligence information as well as sensitive information about military strategy, it should disclose basic information about the scope of the drone program, the legal basis for the program, and the civilian casualties that have resulted from the program."

The SCOPE? To kill Islamists. Legal basis? How about that it's a War Zone? Civilian casualties?---the ACLU has never been concerned about the use of civilians as human shields by Islamists. The U.S. military does everything possible to avoid civilian casualties. Unfortunately, there is that "War Zone" issue. And Islamists who use civilians as human shields. Oh, and the fact that this is occurring in other countries, ones which are not American, How about just butting out ACLU. Go bug some grammar school in Alabama because they had an evil Santa statue at Christmas time. JEEZ.

A Blatant Attempt to Socialize America

"Socialism" like the ancient ideas from which it springs, confuses the distinction between Government and Society". As a result of this, every time we object to a thing being done by government, the Socialist conclude that we object to its being done at all. As a result of an insidious "Progressive" move by the Democratic Party and the President to make the Federal Government the largest employer in the country, the leftwing media has managed to paint all objection to this Socialist plan as non-progressive pathetic attempts to support the free-enterprise system in this country. It is a system it totally despises and is attempting to undermine.

Anyone who fails to see this everyday in our major newspapers and television networks, is not paying attention. Where is the objection to over 70% of new job creation going to labor unions and Government jobs this year? And just where are the "new" jobs being created that puts meals on the table of the Average American in this country? Why did Congress adjourn before extending unemployment payments to10 million men and women still unable to find a job before the funds ran out?

The average worker in this country never gives "Socialism" the slightest thought in his day to day existence. That worker never associates unemployment pay with any form of socialism simply because he does not associate the Federal Government with giving him anything. As far as he is concerned, that money comes from his own contributions, through payroll taxes.---Besides, at the State level, it is the employer that is paying for this program. As a former business owner myself, I can tell you that in this State the EDD collects nearly a billion dollars a year from employers to fund this system.

What we have, in regard to this President, is a blatant attempt to Socialize this country. Now I am sure that I will hear from a certain progressive faction regarding this article and it will not be complimentary. Non-the-less, it is a fact. If someone here in Benicia has solid facts that refute what

I am writing, please let me hear from you. (I am sure the Editor would love to read your comments.)

The president has consistently denied that he is a Socialist, an ideologue, or a "talking head" as some have identified him. The fact is: he is all the above and a lot more than I won't get into today. When one begins to seriously sift through all the "facts" of his campaigns and his 18 months in the White House, one comes to the same conclusion as Thomas Sowell, a wonderful columnist in the Washington Post. He said recently (Vallejo Times Herald 6/22/10) "This government is not governing. It is about creating an impression. That worked on the campaign trail in 2008, but it is a disaster in the White House, where rhetoric is no substitute for reality".

Political theorists seldom agree on anything. But in the case of Obama's attempt to turn this country into a Pan-European Socialist State; the general consensus is it will not work in this country now, or at anytime in the future. This is compounded by the realization that we are not likely to see another president like this one for a long, long time.

Men of this ilk are not born, they are manufactured. Think about that one for a while my friends.

Afghanistan—It Is Time T Leave

Sandwiched between Iran and Pakistan to the West and the East and the former USSR States of Turkmenistan and Tajikistan to the North, Afghanistan is about as remote an area that exists on this earth. For thousands of years, European powers as far back as Alexander, have tried to conquer this wild and mountainous land without success.

Few Americans had ever heard of this country prior to its invasion and occupation by the USSR which ended on February 15, 1989. Following that withdrawal, the country fell into a horrendous civil war that continues to this day. Years after the Russian withdrawal, and following the attack on 9/11, the Bush Administration, with the approval of Congress, attacked Afghanistan and still remains there.

With that background out of the way, we can begin to talk about the story of the Taliban and Al Qaeda and the war in Afghanistan that nearly no one in this country is aware of. And hopefully, I can bring some sense of reality to this war that continues to defy it.

I will begin by saying that it is time to leave Afghanistan. This decision has been a long time coming. I have come to the realization that we can no longer justify the death of a single American soldier protecting Afghanistan. There is simply no intelligent reason for it.

When we first went into Afghanistan, we did so with a purpose. It was a good war of retribution and it was, from a military standpoint, do-able and necessary. It no longer meets any of those standards and it is time we were out of there. As far as I can discern, the only thing we are doing at this point, other than getting our boys killed, is protecting poppy fields and a devious and highly untrustworthy President (Karzi) and his drug lord brother.

Additionally, we are slowly destroying everything that is Afghan that the tribes haven't already destroyed themselves. The Afghans have not once thanked us and nor should they. Or will they ever.

What has happened in Afghanistan since the withdrawal of the Russian army in 1989 is a story of religion, wholesale killing, desperation, and the arrival of a tall Saudi who followers called the "Emir". Following the Soviet withdrawal, the warlords simply disintegrated into a patchwork quilt of snarling, feuding, self serving opportunists who, far from uniting to form a stable government, did the reverse. They created a civil war.

Then something of importance happened in the Afghan South. Since the fall of any semblance of a central government, the old official Afghan Army had simply reassigned itself to the local warlord who paid the best. Outside Kandahar, some soldiers took two teenage girls back to the camp and raped them.

The local preacher in the village nearby, who also ran his own religious school, went to the Army camp with thirty of his students and sixteen rifles. Against all odds, they trounced the soldiers and hanged the Commandant from the canon barrel of his tank. The priest was called Mohammad Omar or Mulla Omar. He had lost his right eye in battle.

The news spred quickly. Others appealed to him for help and the group swelled in numbers, and responded to the appeals. They took no money, they raped no women, they stole no crops, they asked for no reward. They became local heroes. By December 1994, twelve thousand had joined them, adopting the Mullah's black turban. They called themselves the students. In the Padhto dialect "student" is "**talib**" and the plural is "**Taliban**". From village vigilantes, they became a movement and when they captured the city of Kandahar, an alternative government.

The Taliban army has never been a real army. It has no commanding generals, no general staff, no officer corps, no ranks and no infrastructure. Each small area is a individual world of its own and the only world that most of these people have ever known. Each **lashkar** is independent under its tribal leader who often holds sway through personality and courage in combat, plus religious devotion. Before 9/11, most people had never heard of Osama Bin Laden. Amazingly, in some remote areas, they still haven't.

Mullah Omar was a warrior priest but nothing more. Having started his revolution by hanging a rapist from a gun barrel, he withdrew into seclusion in his southern fortress, Kandahar. His followers were something out of the Middle Ages, and among the many things they could not recognize was fear. They worshipped the one eyed Mullah behind his walls. Before the Taliban fell to the Northern Alliance of Tajik Shah Massound, eighty thousand would die for him.

At that time, the tall Saudi "Emir", Osama Bin Laden, now controlled more than twenty thousand Arabs in the mountains of Afghanistan.

The introduction of American forces into this madhouse began in 2001 and consisted originally of tremendous deadly air attacks from submarines and destroyers.

Most of this hell and destruction came from two missile cruisers **Cowpen** and **Shiloh** in the Red Sea, and from the destroyers **Briscoe, Elliot, Hayler, Milius** and the submarine **Columbia**, all in the Arabian Gulf south of Pakistan. The missles were aimed at the training camps of Al Qaeda and the caves of the Tora Bora.

Whole mountains were destroyed and filled valleys that once supported agrarian communities with herds of goats, sheep, and cattle which were the lifeblood of entire tribes. But they didn't kill the tall Emir, Osama Bin Laden. They did, however, manage to kill thousands of Al Qaeda fighters. Today, Al Qaeda is pretty much destroyed but the Taliban is there and still doing what they do best, kill and subvert the tribes of the region.

And we are there and we are still doing what we now do best; asking permission before we shoot at people who are killing us and acting as targets for just about everyone. And no one seems to know why we are there., well….not exactly. We are told it is to prevent Al Qaeda from attacking us again….really? At last count there were something like 50 Al Qaeda in Afghanistan. And…as far as I can determine, the Taliban is not planning attacks around the world. What they are primarily interested in is protecting their poppy fields and Osama is no hero to the Taliban. According to most of their leaders, he is the one that has caused most of their misery, not us.

So when I sat down recently and began to think of Afghanistan and the deaths of our young men and women and attempted to balance their deaths against what we are accomplishing over there------- the decision was easy. Get our boys out of there, Mr. President. Eleven years is enough, sir. The far left and the Afghanistan people hate us for our presence there and the conservatives can live with a pull out. I know I can. Just declare victory and leave.

Answers From The Street

Have you seen one of the "Man on the Street" interviews lately? There have been quite a few recently asking questions in regard to politics and politicians. The level of ignorance shown in regard to this subject is staggering. It makes one wonder just how we can elect politicians (and presidents) when the electorate, is for the most part, totally unaware of what is going on in this country.

It begs the question: Should there be an exam to pass before you can be registered to vote? The truth be known, that is why we are a Republic. When the nation was founded, the founding fathers realized that the average education of the population at that time was nearly non-existent. Simply put, they could not be trusted to make decisions regarding the management of this country.

It almost seems that way today. It explains why our country is in the shape we are in. If a candidate has enough money, he can buy an office in Washington or Sacramento, or any other location in America. 2008 was a fine example of what I am Saying. Look at the scenario. In that election year, the Democratic Party nominated a relatively young black man that nearly no one had ever heard of outside of Chicago. He was however, supported by a massive amount of campaign money furnished by an eclectic combination of billionaires, labor unions, and the very wealthy that thought it was a cool thing to do. (Can you say San Francisco?) Plus a media hell bent on electing him, no questions asked.

During that campaign year, there was a series of "man in the street" interviews done in television networks, comedy shows (they were very funny) and the local media. In nearly all of these interviews the "man in the street" appears as a uninformed "dummy". To be fair, a great number of us would be hard pressed to answer some of these questions, but on the whole, the performances were frightening dismal and absolutely depressing.

One of those shows which ran on the Fox News Network (you know the uber right wing one) took place on the campus at U.C. Berkeley. Now one would expect that the students at Berkeley would have been much more informed than the average "man on the street". Well...if you thought that, you were wrong. The average answers were no more correct than the answers you would expect from the street.

Today we are looking at the possibility of a presidential campaign by Donald Trump. The liberal press and mainstream television networks are having a field day with this and dismissing Mr. Trump as a "joke" candidate, How is Mr. Trump anymore a "joke" candidate that Mr, Obama was in 2008.

The fact is...he is not. The truth be known, Trump is someone that the majority of people (voters) are familiar with. Mr. Trump is a tremendously successful real estate investor and is known around the world as a very smart man and an extraordinary negotiator. Mr. Obama was in 2008, a junior U.S. Senator with less than two years in office and had no other work experience other than as a part time lecturer at the University of Chicago and a "community organizer". Practically speaking, no one knew anything about this young man other than the people in the Chicago area.

I am not going to comment on the attempt by Mr. Trump to use the "birther" insinuations as an entry method into the campaign, but he is probably one of the very few who had the gravitas to do it. The press in this country has wasted no time in attacking Mr. Trump, or in some cases ignoring Mr. Trump. The point I am attempting to make here is this: Here we go again! Once more the media in this country is attempting to control the outcome of a Presidential election. Trump is every bit as qualified (actually more qualified) as Obama was in 2008. It is not likely that Trump can get the Republican nomination, and I doubt he would attempt to run as an Independent, but what is happening with the media is obscene. When did voters in America begin to allow the press to pick our President? Was it in 2008? It is beginning to look that way.

In 2008, the press did everything possible to elect Obama. It is actually impossible to deny it. Now two years later, they are attempting to do it again. But this time Mr. Obama is not the clean slate he was in 2008. On this day, his numbers in some polls are in the low 40 percentiles. This time it is going to be much harder to do what they did in 2008. And this brings us back to the "man in the street". Unfortunately, the man in the street has not gotten any smarter. Thirty second news bites are often good enough to get most any idea across to these people. In the case of Labor Unions, even 30 second news bites are not necessary to get the job done. Union members vote as they are told to vote. Union members financially support candidates chosen by their unions (no questions asked.

Where are the intelligent voters of the past in this country? Actually, where are all the smart, educated, involved people of past elections? I can't answer that question because I just don't know. But....I do know this: our education has gone down so badly as to be nearly of no consequence, How can we expect to have an electorate that is capable of electing capable and honest candidates when most of these people don't even know who the candidates are? Don't laugh, just for the fun of it, ask someone you work with or do business with who the Attorney General of California is today. Or even better, ask them to name the members of the Benicia City Council, or the new City Manager. You may be shocked at the answers.

Climate Gate—it is not over

Is anyone reading this aware that while in Copenhagen during the Climate Change Conference, President Obama made a pledge to provide 100 billion dollars over the next 10 years to third world countries mostly in Africa?

There are several things going on here in regard to that pledge. First there was not a mention of this in the mainline media. The president had absolutely no authority to make that pledge without the authorization of Congress. He didn't have it and thus the pledge is worth nothing. By making that pledge, Obama was able to escape Copenhagen with just some egg on his face and not the whole omelet,. He must realize however, that he has raised the Oz curtain just enough to expose a glimpse of the real Wizard. Given the condition of this economy, there is a snow balls chance in Hades that a congressional authorization will ever come.

Has anyone seen our very large Academy Award winning ex-vice President lately? I didn't think so. Since canceling his extravagant ($2,000 a plate) dinner in Copenhagen, Fat Albert has gone basically into hiding. And why do you think he might want to do that? How about the fact that his net worth was recently announced and it approaches half a billion dollars? I find nothing wrong with that other than most of that money came from his investments in green technology and a climate crisis he created.

The failure of the president to produce some dramatic announcement at the conference did nothing to salvage his shrinking popularity and prestige in Europe and around the world. But, folks, everything he has done or said in the last two years has been all smoke and mirrors. If he were anywhere near as bright and resolute as he has been made out to be, he would never have promised time and time again, that which he knew he was unlikely to be able to produce.

Jim Pugh

Today, left with some chance of passing this God awful health bill and little else, this president has gone on a 2-3 day a week speech tour that borders on near hysterics. His pathological promises during election in 2008 are coming home (as Rev. Wright said) to roost. And don't forget, the Greenies expect him to save the world! It ain't over yet folks---not by a long shot.

The White House- Union Shop

On June 11th, columnist George Will wrote in a column for Newsmax.Com, President Obama is sacrificing economic growth and job creation in order to placate organized labor. And, ad the crisis of the welfare deepens, he is trying to enlarge the entitlement system and exacerbate the entitlement mentality.

This statement is, without a doubt, an absolute fact. Forty four Republican Senators, three more than necessary to stop Senate action, have vowed to block confirmation of John Bryson. He is the President's nominee to be Commerce Secretary, until the President submits for Congressional approval, the already negotiated free-trade agreements with South Korea, Panama, and Columbia.

The 44 are responding to this: President Obama, since he took office, has continuously laid down for organized labor and has made no effort to deny that fact. The latest example of this is the support the Obama White House is giving to a suit against Boeing Aircraft by organized labor in South Carolina. So please understand. South Carolina is a "right to work" state. A worker in South Carolina cannot be forced to join a labor union in order to get a job and a company cannot be forced to allow a labor union to organize its workforce.

The people of South Carolina voted to amend its Constitution to make this possible. At this time, the National Labor Relations Board has taken on the sovereign State of South Carolina in an attempt to challenge the constitutionality of that amendment.

And why do you suppose the NLRB wants to do this so badly? Simple…it is a blatant attempt to stop Boeing from building a new plant in Charleston and hiring 2,000 non-union workers.

Let us stop for a moment and look at the make-up of the NLRB. This board is composed of members appointed by the president. Presently, one of these members is a "back door" appointee who has not been approved by the Senate. This member gives the President control of the board. Although he claims to have no such authority, he has appointed every one of these members. Obama states that he cannot legally tell this board what to do, but, come on folks…he owns the NLRB as it is presently configured.

The result of all this is another example of the vast amount of power and influence Labor has on this administration. Simply put, this President desperately needs the support of organized labor to be elected in November 2012. In order to get this support, Barrack Obama is willing to knuckle under to Labor demands nationwide.

From its inception, this administration has trumpeted it's admiration of the European style of Socialism and is more than willing to put Labor in a controlling position., if Labor reciprocates by giving Obama the vast majority of its votes at the polls. This is a pure symbiotic relationship and similar relationships in Europe have nearly destroyed the European Union.

What is happening to England and Greece today is the inevitable future of Obama style economics. There is no escape from this destiny. It is only a matter of time. What happens when a large number of people depend upon the government for their livelihood, through Union demands, public employment and welfare? The government must naturally grow larger to provide for these people. It must seize more funding from the private sector. It would fund the salaries and benefits of public employees, overpaid Union members, and finance welfare for the dependency class. It must hire more people to administer these vast new funds…. and their salaries must be paid.

Every government is either the ally, or the enemy of law abiding private citizens. The sole factor controlling that relationship is the size of the State. A huge government will always be the enemy if its' people, because those who depend on the government will eventually, and inevitably, insist upon it. What is happening in Europe today is the absolute forerunner of what will happen in this country should this administration be allowed to continue down this path to European Socialism.

I find it nearly impossible to believe that the electorate in this country has sunken to this level of ignorance or indifference, or a combination of both. The presidential elections of 2012 will be, without hesitation, the most important in the history of the United States. No doubt about it folks!!

Situational Ethics

I have said repeatedly, that in my opinion we are not going to solve the economic and moral problems facing our nation anytime in the near future. Strong words, but true. To do so would require a moral fiber that is virtually non-existent in politics (and in society) today. The combination of welfare, government handouts, and a steady barrage of "situational ethics" training in the public schools makes real reform all but impossible, barring a true ethics revival.

Government 'entitlement' programs, along with over-regulation, are sucking the life's blood out of the economy and making more and more Americans actually believe that more government spending can solve our economic problems. We have created a situation in which solutions are theoretically possible but politically impossible, eventually economic chaos, which dictates our concern over unemployment, business failures, and the loss of homes, overshadows the concern about diminishing individual rights of the voters, who have sought a political savior. The problem is: this "Savior" has turned out to be hardly the miracle man he was once thought to be. In reality, he has expanded, if not actually created more of these problems than he has solved. It is very possible, should the crisis get anymore serious, the majority of Americans will vote away a large portion of their individual freedoms in order to restore some or at least a semblance of our former successes.

The generation of Americans below the age of 60 cannot totally comprehend the realties of a worldwide financial crisis, except in books, movies, or by word of mouth which are not the equivalent of real life experiences. We are brewing up a financial crisis on a scale that makes that depression of the thirties look like a minor dip in the market. Never in the history of economics has a nation as wealthy and influential as this one attempted to live so far beyond its means, while simultaneously electing a president who is doing everything politically possible to strangle our economy. This is the

Obama economical plan in a nut shell. But, you can't distribute wealth by making the rich poor, and this seems to be the core of his plan.

California is the prime example of what is happening to this nation. Our business base (which supports everything else) is being burdened to the point that a new enterprise is difficult or impossible to start successfully. Even established businesses are having a near impossible time of coping with all the rules and regulations that have made this state the most difficult in the union in regard to business start ups, Forty years ago there were few other places for our entrepreneurs to go if they were dissatisfied with start up requirements. Today any number of countries will offer them unlimited capital, lower taxes, and fewer regulations. Even other states (Nevada as a prime example) have laid down the welcome mat to California industry. The man in the Oval Office should take a strong look at this state before he thinks of following our example.

This administration appears to have no idea how to handle this crisis, that for the most part, they have created. Please don't start with the worn out "it is the Republicans' fault". It has been nearly two years since Obama took office. Every single bill that this administration has rammed through congress has simply made things worse.

If we don't succeed in forcing some quick changes within a few years, this government will exhaust all of the available money in our economy. Even if this president had the resolve (and he doesn't) to attempt to balance the budget, he lacks the constitutional authority to do so. Those in this government that derive their support base by spending other peoples' money won't stop until (and unless) they have no other choice. It is simple enough to list senators and congressmen and women – who consistently vote to spend more every year, and vote them out of office, this year or at the time they must stand for re-election.

You must first understand and believe the problem exists, then you have to write and call to voice your opinion. Remember that there are many good people in Washington who will vote for what is right if we can just convince them. The evidence is on our side and the power to re-elect is ours.

We just need them to listen to the voice of reason and the American people. Should that fail) and that is surely possible) then we should send them all home and start over again. It starts this fall and it is absolutely necessary that we do what only as American voters have the power to do, restore the greatest country on earth to its former place of leadership in this world. Third world countries do not have the power to be that--------do they?

The Great Copenhagen Ilumination

On December 9, 2009, politicized scientists were joining the politicians who funded them to commence 12 days of deceptive global warming propaganda designed to trash capitalism and to promote more regulation, higher taxes, global governance, and global redistribution of wealth.

Anyone who believed that this country could afford to contribute a billion dollars a year each, to countries such as Bangladesh, Indonesia, and a bevy of central African countries (for god knows what reason) was not gifted with a great deal of intelligence.

At that time, a year before we found ourselves facing 10% unemployment, the largest national deficient in our nations' history, and possible double digit inflation, how on earth did this president think that we could afford to fund the global redistribution of wealth? In addition, given the data scandal that was going on, there was no overwhelming evidence that global warming actually existed in any meaningful way. There still isn't.

The very same researchers caught secretly e-mailing one another about how they rigged global temperature records were among the most prominent scientist framing that had come out of the Intergovernmental Panel on Climate Change (IPCC) on which all the Copenhagen doomsday predictions were based. Given all this, the Copenhagen meeting should have been canceled, at least until a whole new set of uncontaminated and honest data could be compiled and evaluated, which could take 10 years or more.

These so called climate "scientists" e-mails revealed that they had been destroying or altering data when the measurements didn't support their point of view. As a result, absolutely nothing they said could be considered trustworthy. Everything they had published should have been thrown out and new research should have begun again with new researchers. It was not.

Al Gore, the driving force behind this bogus science, should have been stripped of the huge amount of money he had made through this global warming fraud and had it redistributed to his victims, the ones forced to pay higher fuel and energy bills and more for almost everything else they bought because of new climate policies and regulations.

Anyone who has paid any attention to the global warming issue knew long ago that we were being lied to when a prominent climate scientist urged colleagues to "offer up scary scenarios" and make public statements without mentioning the doubts and uncertainties they had about "global warming".

And we would continue to be lied to that week by other socialist politicians in Copenhagen, by scientists they bankrolled, and by the liberal media that had told you little or nothing about the e-mails that suggested global warming was a manipulated pseudoscientific fraud that should have led to the firing of every scientist ever vaguely involved in it. It didn't, but no surprise there.

By distorting science to create an ideological agenda, Mr. Gore had destroyed whatever authority and credibility that he possessed when scientist began their research. By that same logic, with global warming being used to promote bigger government and higher taxes, we should have found the gumption to ask Mr. Gore straight on to explain how he had accumulated nearly 287 million dollars in his personal bank account. Now that, my friends, would be a very interesting conversation, particularly given he has lost a huge amount of it in the last 15 months.

Despite all of this, we are still surrounded by a bevy of "Climate Control" experts who continue to beat that same drum with enthusiasm. It is amazing that just in this past week we have seen several articles written by apparently intelligent individuals that simply will not admit that their Guru, Albert Gore, and his followers around the world, were dead wrong on December 9, 2009, just as they are today.

Somali Refugees

Very recently, the State Department accepted, with the president's consent, 6,000 Somali refugees who were located in camps in Uganda. I am sure you were not aware that. I certainly was not until I read of it in David Limbaugh's excellent new book CRIMES AGAINST LIBERTY. And why was this done?

Well….according to a United Nations Organization, the reason they are being moved is their failure to integrate with other refugee groups and their tendency to rally toward jihadist among them. Would someone please explain how on God's green earth this was allowed to happen at this time in this country, a time when we are going through a severe recession and when our country is the target of every terrorist organization in the world?

Folks, there is an undercurrent of over the top progressive thought among certain operatives in the West Wing that even the president is possibly not aware. Not to say that this man would necessarily oppose such thoughts or actions. The very fact that our State Department would even consider such an obviously ill advised move such as this Somali affair, indicates that this faction in the West Wing has become incredibly influential and are able to make such things possible.

Do you think that there may have been any clear thought involved in a decision to move 6,000 Somali, many who are clearly Jihadi into this country? What possible good was this to anyone, Somali or anyone in America? These people, who have proven while in Uganda, to be a singular problem to the United Nations, are supposed to fit neatly into American society?

Nothing could be further from the truth. Yet this was done with the approval of Hillary Clinton and the president. Neither you, I, nor anyone else outside of the administration knew anything of this. There was not a peep from any major network including Fox, and not a single newspaper in the country printed a word of this.

I have not been able to find anything regarding these 6,000 people or when they were moved or where they went. Unfortunately, there is nothing in Limbaugh's book that follows up on their whereabouts at this time. Even this was odd. Why mention it at all if he was not going to follow up on the location? Where on earth do you put 6,000Africans without someone being aware of them? Strange business this.

It is, of course, perfectly feasible that this country simply assumed responsibility for these people and have moved them to another country in Africa. Where that could possibly be is a total mystery. Where do you put 6,000Africans that include terrorist factions? According to Limbaugh, the agreement was for the Somalis to go to this country. It appears that this has not occurred yet. Even this highly bias, progressive media could not hide that happening. The simple fact is this: this administration assumes that it does not fall with the parameters of common sense actions. What makes sense in regard to these people does not include moving them into this country. Where do you put them? It is a very simple question. Do you send them into the Nevada desert or somewhere in desolate central Texas? Wherever it is, it must be isolated.

Let's face it, it simply doesn't work. It can't be made workable and someone as intelligent as Hillary Clinton surely must be aware of that. I cannot for the life of me understand how these things happen. Surely someone other that Clinton made that decision. I don't believe it was the president, either. The West Wing is full of suspects, unidentified individuals whose agenda is hidden from view but appears on occasion such as this. There is an element in this White House that seems to operate on it's own will. This appears to be one of those times.

Sometimes the Truth is Painful

Today on the 19th of September, the San Francisco Chronicle, in an editorial by Editor John Diaz, reflected it continual support of Barack Obama for good or bad. It was the first peep out of Diaz since the debacle hit the airwaves and the editorial pages of newspapers everywhere.

The editorial, through a continuous and torturous explanation of the facts (at least as he interpreted them) Diaz extracted the truth according to Barack. His truth?... The president was at worst, just an unfortunate victim of circumstance. The president was unaware of the actual financial condition of Solyndra, and was misled by the subordinates.

The fact that one of the president's busiest bundlers during his initial election to the White House, George Kaiser (one of the largest investors), visited the White House on behalf of Solyndra four times shortly before the loan guarantee was issued, seemed to have escaped Diaz's attention. What does this president, and the Democratic Party, for that matter, have to do to get negative attention from John Diaz?

This loan guarantee was the result of simple political hanky panky on behalf of the Obama administration. Obama desperately needed a positive poster child for the solar panel industry that the West Wing was pushing so fervently (can you say Van Jones?) The Bush administration, after diligent examination, had rejected the loan guarantee just weeks before Obama took office, saying that the company (Solyndra) was a year late and more than a few dollars short of being a viable operation.

But, that did not stop Jones and company from renewing the application and pushing the president for its approval. And…that is what he did. There are no records that the president did anything but respond in a positive way to Jones and open the cash drawer to a corporation that had one foot in the grave and which folded less than fifteen months later. No due diligence here by Obama or anyone else. This was politics at its worse.

97

But…Mr. Diaz made no mention of this or any other aspect of this, only that the administration had not been aware, at the time of the application, of the desperate condition of Solydra's finances. Why, for God's sake didn't they know? This is a fair question, but one that is not being asked by the major media in this country, the Chronicle included. Obviously, Diaz is not interested in the actual facts of this case, only in attempting to put the best face on a disaster for the White House.

The visits by Mr. Kaiser appear not to be regarded, by the White House, as anything but business as usual. John Diaz is an ideologist. Diaz is not particularly interested in any of the facts unless those facts support his ideology. He simply refuses to look at this president in any negative way.

We must take a step back and look at how this could effect our little town and its' love affair with solar energy. Just as the Obama administration claims to have been hoodwinked by not so honest individuals in the solar energy business, there are indications that on a smaller scale, the same thing could very well occur right here in Benicia.

This begs the question: What private company/corporation is the big beneficiary of this solor construction, (probably something I should know already) and why does all of this seem to be coming out of nowhere? Why is this such a big surprise? Could it be that most of the residents of our little town were just not paying attention? I could be one of those. But…I wonder how many, had they been aware, would be in favor of cutting down two stands of beautiful healthy trees? Especially since we have just recently purchase and planted 100 new trees in the city.

Like with every other new technology, we don't know just how well that solar project is going to be performing in ten years, provided that it will still be in operation. We simply have no guarantees that it will be. What happened to our "Solar Village" which was built around 20 years ago? The homes are still there, but they are not solar powered any longer and haven't been for a very long time.

What I am saying here is this, we must, unlike the Obama administration, do our "due diligence" and make sure that what we are building today will be serving us 20 years from now. Please think about that. There appears to be a rabid groundswell of "build green" that has enveloped the mind set of a great many people here in Benicia. It all sounds wonderful, and GREEN… but it is just not practical at this time, if it will ever be. I know I will hear from those that hold strongly to their belief that it will, but the facts are the facts and they don't support this huge move toward solar at this time. Maybe someday, but now is not that time.

The Press and the Truth

On he 21st of March, the Democrat majority in Congress passed the Obama Healthcare Reform Bill. Not a single Republican member of Congress voted "yes" on that bill. In early 1940, Winston Churchill stated at the beginning of the bombing of London, "Now this is not the end. It is not even the beginning of the end. But, it is, perhaps the end of the beginning." If you are following the hoopla regarding this victory in the mainstream press, then you are convinced that this "historic victory" is equated to passing the Civil Rights Bill, Social Security, or even Medicare, all wrapped up in one.

But, unlike Social Security and Medicare, which were both popular bills that were passed with large bipartisan majorities, this bill was unpopular, passed without Republican support, and most of the benefits don't come into effect until 2014. The simple fact is, the majority of people in this country do not like the bills. A week before the final vote, polls showed up to 73% of the public were not in favor of the bill as they understood it to be (no one had seen it). And yet…mainstream media, ignoring these polls entirely, spoke of the Obama Healthcare bill as if it was the greatest thing since sliced bread and… Obama was the baker.

Well…it is not. Just as it has during the last 3 years, the media is out to convince the American public that this president, who just over 3 years ago, no one had ever heard of, had suddenly emerged as the brightest, most educated, and resourceful politician since Lincoln. Well…he is not. Notice that they have yet to say that he was the most experienced. Not even the New York Times would venture to go that far. The truth is Barack Obama is the most unprepared president this country has ever elected. That is fact and simply cannot be denied by anyone willing to look at reality.

A majority of Americans, but obviously not including those of our mainstream media, could see through all the procedural tricks like reconciliation and the "deeming votes" and special deals to boggle the imagination. There was no need to rush the vote through before the bill's cost could be thoroughly analyzed and digested. Contrary to what most Democratic politicians believe, a vast majority could see through all of this. They aren't stupid. But, apparently the Democrats believed that many of them are—they simply didn't understand the beneficence of the legislation that the Democrats were prepared to force on them, presumably for their own good. As for the rest of us, it seems they think that we wickedly opposed a bill that would benefit others for nothing more than our own selfish reasons. Can a president successfully govern a nation when he apparently believes that a majority of its citizens are either stupid or evil? We shall see.

One thing, however, is certain: In a dazzling irony, through the ugly procedural "reform" drama in which he has embroiled the country, the most enthusiastically pro-government president in recent American history has demonstrated once and for all just how corrupt, cynical and inept our government can be, when lead by a Machiavellian leader driven by ambition and a steady resolve.

This was a power grab, pure and simple, and a little bit of what has made this a great country, died on the floor of the House Sunday night. And as Speaker Pelosi and her lieutenants walked arm and arm in triumph in front of the Capitol building Monday, celebrating their historic victory, the national mainstream media cheered and cheered and a good time was had by all. Legislative chicanery, bribery, and utter distain for the will of people had won the day.

The Law and the Left

Like it or not, judicial activism is with us to stay. Advocating judicial restraint now, given the current state of American law, is akin to trying to fight a modern war with seventeenth-century weapons. Allowing the left to pillage our cities with the weapons of judicial activism while we stand throwing the flowers of judicial restraint in their way is a path to dismal failure. A new tactic is required.

Like all real conservatives, I pride myself on being a hard-core political realist--on being rational, knowing history, understanding economics and human nature, and looking at the world as it really is, not as I would wish it to be. The Right, after all, takes a reality-based approach to life, society, and politics.

What males Liberals realists when it comes to American law? The Left is results—oriented, while the Right follows the path of process. Look how Liberal evaluates judges. The judges they praise the most are the ones who have handed them policy victories. You almost never hear the Left praising a judge's legal reasoning or interpretative methods, except perhaps as an afterthought; all that matters are the results of the judge's decisions—the political ramifications of those rulings in the real world.

For example, National Public Radio's Juan Williams hails Justice Thurgood Marshall for promoting "preferences, set-asides, and other race-conscious policies" as the remedy for the damage remaining from the "history of slavery and racial bias." This response from William is a typical reaction of those who never cease to blame race for the failure of minorities in this country. Marshal was of the school of legal minds sought out by the Left. Those that not only espoused the Liberal doctrine, but were in the position to turn it into law.

The Left's emphasis on the political and social policy results of a particular legal decision came to the forethought during the Senate confirmation hearing of Chief Justice John Roberts. Senator Dick Durbin pressed the nominee for his view on a Supreme Court decision that required state taxpayers to pay free public schooling for the children of illegal immigrants. Needless to say, nothing in the Constitution required state taxpayer in California to provide a free education to the kids of illegal immigrants—yet the Supreme Court interpreted the Constitution to say exactly that.

Still, Senator Durbin explained to Roberts, "Whether we're talking millions of uninsured people or millions of Hispanic children, I would like to think it would be a basic value, you would say that this is good for America for people to have insurance and bad for them to be denied; it is good for America to see children with education rather than to see them in the streets, ignorant. It seems so fundamental".

Roberts's response, typical of mainstream conservative legal thought, indicated a much different sense of the role of the law, and the courts: "Senator, I don't think you want judges who will decide cases before them under the law on what they think is good—simply good policy for America. There are legal questions there. Were it our business to set the nation's social policy, I would agree without hesitation that it is senseless for an enlightened Society to deprive any children—including illegal aliens—of an elementary education…However, the Constitution does not constitute us as 'Platonic Guardians' nor does it vest in this Court the authority to strike down laws because they do not meet our standards of desirable social policy, 'wisdom' or 'common sense'.

Simply put, conservatives view the Left as a bunch of wild-eyes utopians beholden to harebrained schemes and fantasies that can work only in the imagination of some nebbish sociology professor with too much time on his hands. But in the debate over the courts—the Elana Kagan nomination being a prime example—it's the conservatives who become the wild-eyes utopians and the liberal who operate as the realist. The Left long ago recognized that courts are political institutions that can be used to further a political agenda. The Right, in contrast, refuses to accept the inevitable. Failing to recognize that the courts long ago became politicized, it embraces flawed notions such as judicial restraint and strict constructionism. Conservatives demand a return to a world in which courts play a limited role in American government and politics. But, that is pure fantasy. We can never get back to that world. Sure, it would be lovely if courts didn't practice judicial activism, but we must accept the courts as they are—political institutions with extraordinary power to invent rights not mentioned in the Constitution, to overturn democratically enacted laws, to make law and to change law.

The recent decision by the high court regarding Christian Law Club at the Hastings School of Law in San Francisco, is just the last of an ongoing series of legal opinion of judges that feel absolutely no compulsion to follow the letter of the law as they have in the past. So it is. So it will continue. The spirit of the law as we know it, will cease to exist, if it hasn't already. As is the law of 50 years ago—it is no longer relevant in the legal scheme of things. The law is an ongoing process that continues to follow its own path and the morals of man. Given the condition of society today, we are in for a rough rode. And as a side note: the Christian Law Club decision was bad law, judicial activism be damned.

Who Are these People in Washington?

Ten days ago, Barrack Obama named Andrew Stern the President of the Service Employees international Union (SEIU) to the newly created Deficient Reduction Commission. This commission is so new that there is very little known about it other than what its' name indicates.

Can someone possibly explain to me just what males Stern qualified to serve on such a commission? Given his education (Bachelors Degree in Urban Planning from the University of Pennsylvania and a certificate in whatever from the "Midwest Academy", a school that trains leftist community organizers to infiltrate labor unions), serving on that commission will be a stretch of his budgeting ability.

As far as I can determine, Stern is no more qualified to serve on that commission (DRC) than the manager of our local Safeway store. He is, however, the personal Guru to our President. Given that Obama himself has absolutely zero business experience or any executive experience whatsoever, has never made a payroll or created a budget or any kind, never failed to vote yea on any spending bill while in the Senate, he also appears not qualified to sit on that commission.

Then too, no one seems to be able to define just what the commission actually does. I don't seem to be able to find anything that describes exactly what the DRC has been asked to do or what the qualifications are for membership. Reducing the deficit seems fairly self explanatory, but we don't need a commission to do that, that is a job of our legislature and the President. Perhaps the President has lost faith in Congress, but surely not in himself, that would be beyond imagination.

It appears to me that Obama has simply found another plum to gift his favorite guy. After all, the 44 visits Stern made to the White House last year must have strengthened that extraordinary bond the two men have with each other. Lacking an appropriate board or commission that suits Mr. Stern, the President simply created one for him.

A couple of weeks ago, Stern declared, "The SEIU had spent $165 million on the election of Barrack Obama, and in support of his programs… even more. Now it's time the SEIU received something in return".

This is a man confident of his position in the White House pecking order. Such talk has given the press an indication that Obama is in the pocket of the SEIU. I have a feeling, however, being place on an obscure commission that on one every heard of is not going to make Stern willing to call things even.

The behind closed doors deal made with the Union in which the Union was exempted from taxes on "Cadillac Plans" was not offered to small businesses or anyone else not offering up huge amounts of money in return. It would appear that was a very nice gift to the SEIU even if Stern did not think it adequate. The entire shad y mess that has been the "Healthcare Debate" has been a total disaster for the President. Buying off Senators and paying back unions has been handled so badly it begs the question: Who are these people we have sent to Washington?

The Bush War vs. The Obama War

Recently, a good friend here in Benicia remarked on the absence of the "No War" group in front of the Gazebo in City Park. It dawned on me that the war we are fighting in Afghanistan is Obamas's war—and therefore not to be protested by this particular group.

Call me old fashioned, but war is war. People fight and die on both sides in any war. Correct wars (those approved by peace organizations) are no less deadly than those that are not. One cannot help but note with a certain cynicism the absence of the protestors carrying "Stop the war, stop the killing" and other "war is wrong" signs on the corner of First and Military streets.

These people- and I am sure there are many well meaning among them- seem to have a selective view of war. Our current president, who took possession of Afghanistan war even before he was elected, has deemed this war "his" and therefore a "correct" war. Well folks, I have to tell you, there is no war more correct than any other. Young men and women die in war. Correct wars are just as deadly and just as brutal as any other.-only the sentiment is different.

So let us try to understand what the "NO War" group is saying by their absence from the park. Are they saying George Bush is evil, so therefore his war must be as well? Barrack Obama is good, so his war must be, too. I am curious about this mind set. Besides being completely nonsensical, it projects a certain elitism that is disturbing. People who look down their noses at those in our military are demeaning the one group in our nation that is responsible for our freedom throughout history.

The American military has never declared war on anyone. They don't because they can't. Wars are declared by Our Congress, and more recently by our Presidents. The American soldier has been trained to follow orders and to do their job. By the very nature of the system, soldiers simply cannot question the authority of the order.

This brings us back to our friends and neighbors who used to stand on the corner of First and Military. Could someone in that group explain their absence since the election of Barrack Obama?

I am just curious. Does this mean that you condone the killing now that Obama is in office? Does the fact that this man is president change the dynamic of the conflict? Could you possibly be so naïve as to believe that?

I am asking you to return. I am asking you to bring your signs and so what you can to put the spotlight back on this "Obama War". If you believe that the lives of our men and women mean anything, come back to the corner. Show the people of this city that killing cannot be selective based on the name of the president ordering it. What you are showing in your absence is that you have little regard for the soldiers- and civilians- dying in Afghanistan today.

What you are showing is that all your protests in the past was not about war and death; it was about George W. Bush- and that is sickening. Come back to the corner.

Within the last few days, the pressure on the president in regard to his good war has increased dramatically. The war in Afghanistan is getting harder and harder to sell. Going there and confronting the Taliban and the terrorists who initiated the attack on this country was a proper war. What has transpired has not. What we had then was a BUSH war. What we have now is an OBAMA war- and this is one you should be protesting, people.

Come back to the corner!

Out of Control President

On the third Tuesday of January 2010, the people of Massachusetts elected a Republican to the U. S. Senate. This was the first time in over five decades that anyone other than democrat has held that seat. Are we seeing a clear trend here?

Could this astounding result be connected in anyway to the major elections of Republicans in Virginia and New Jersey last fall? It's hard to deny with a straight face. The man we have in the White House, and the leaders in the House of Representatives and Senate have for the last year continuously ignored the voters in this country and their arrogance has now been repudiated by the people of the Bay State.

A president has to strike a balance between leading the country and listening to his constituents is always difficult, but rarely has one been so out of touch with people. Americans are overwhelmingly concerned about high unemployment and enormous government deficits. Obama ignored the basic issues, instead choosing to focus upon his own political agenda.

For over a year this president ran around the country preaching transparency and "change" in our government. Over and over again he promised C-SPAN coverage of all bills in Congress. "No more behind closed doors legislation" was his mantra. And yet, after the dust has settled, the doors are still closed—doubled locked would be a better description of what Pelosi and Reid have been doing. Neither the American people nor our elected Representatives and Senators got the chance to review the bills---at least before the votes were taken.

During his campaign in 2008, the president promised a better international image. Well folks---Swedes and Norwegians sure like us better, but has clearly antagonized some of our closest allies (Britain and Israel) and pandered to dictators in North Korea, Iran and Venezuela. At the same time, he nearly gave Honduras to a Chavez front man and has let Columbia hanging out to dry to appease his union buddies.

I have written numerous columns regarding this president. Very few, if any have been complimentary. But honestly, it is not because I simply dislike this man and wish him to fail it is because he has continuously ignored the things he needs to do to make this country safe, successful and a leader in the world.

Our first 'Post American' President has promised to lead us into a new era. Instead he has made constant attempts to take over our banking industry, our auto industry and now our healthcare industry that represents one-sixth of our economy, in the name of saving it. I have been accused of unfairly demeaning this president by some in this community, but honestly folks, he needs to be controlled or we are in for lot worse in the future.

In 1966 I attended a political meeting in the Wade Hampton Hotel in Columbia, South Carolina. It was a gathering of elected officials in the state Republican Party and was held primarily to support Republican congressional candidates. The star of the show was former Vice President Richard Nixon. The room was full of sweat, cigar smoke, and rage. The rhetoric which was about patriotism and law and order, "burned the paint off the walls". As he left the hotel, Nixon is quoted as saying, "This is the future of this Party, right here in the South". He was correct by any standard.

Thirty eight years later, on the night of George W. Bush's second presidential election, the conservative movement seemed indomitable. In fact, it was rapidly falling apart. Conservatives knew how to win elections: however, they turned out not to be very interested in governing. Throughout the decades since Nixon, conservatism has the essentially negative character of an insurgent movement.

Today, we have a relatively young man sitting in the Oval Office. He is all about speeches and campaigns and political cultures of failure. What he is not all about is governing this country. Perhaps he is on the level of "THE ARCHITECT" Karl Rove when it comes to developing campaigns, but he appears to have little or no skill in running this country on a day to day basis. He ran a political campaign in 2008 that will be written about for a longtime into the future. It was chocked full of promises and predictions that were impossible to realize. The disturbing part of all this is:: he was aware of that when he made them.

There are those out there that believe sincerely that this president made those predictions and promises simply to get elected. There are also those that believe he designed his campaign around his own "pie in the sky" fantasy belief that he could make these things happen. Whatever the truth is, this country is in a lot worse shape than it was when he was elected.

This oil spill crisis is a sad indicator of his inability to "get the job done" and his consistent finger pointing and transference of responsibility when things go wrong.

This brings us to his seemingly difficult task of shifting gears after the campaign—from flying frantically around the country giving speeches that someone else has written- to focusing on the problems of state and the health of this country. It is perfectly clear at this time that Mr. Obama has not made that transition easily, if at all, Clearly the speeches and the constant flying are still with us----and not likely to go away anytime soon---if at all. Campaigning is primarily promises---governing is seeing to it that those promises are fulfilled. The promises are the easy part of it. Besides, governing requires a conscience and quite a bit of skill.

Obama 2011 The Third Year

As I have stated in this overview of the year 2011, the interest in that year concentrated (for the most part) in our national obsession on so called "Climate Change" and its effects on the local and national psyche. This aftermath of the Solyndra debacle may have been the single most talked about event of the year.

Around the middle of the year 2011, the National Labor relations Board (NLRB) sought an unprecedented expansion of power to overturn voter approved constitutional amendments in at least two states that guaranteed the secret ballot for union elections. As a side note: in the first two years of the Obama administration, head of the SEIU, Andy Stern was the most frequent visitor to the Oval Office. If there is anyone out there that truly believes that this president is not unduly influenced by big labor, then I have this wonderful little Yugo in the garage that will sell cheap.

Also that year, our president demanded in a television speech that Israel retreat from its current borders to the lines set in 1967. Were we really paying attention?

Book 2011 Titles:

Climate Talks in South Africa: A plea to spend the money

Osama and Obama

Governing by Fiat

What do we call incompetence these days?

The U.A.W. and truth

Following the Osama aftermath

South of the Border

Were We Really Paying Attention?

Solyndra L.L.C. (show me the money)

Time Out

Civil liberties…really?

Elena Kagan Revisited

Obama and the U.N.

Obama's Failure to Perform

No Coming Back

Whether You Like it Or Not

Total Waste of Money

Climate Talks in South Africa: A plea to spend the money

Once again a global climate conference, this on in South Africa, has failed to address the core problems if greenhouse emissions worldwide. But… since the last climate control debacle in Copenhagen, things have actually begun to improve for climate friendly technologies being developed outside the U.N. process.

Still, scientists say they cannot pinpoint exactly when the world's climate will reach a tipping point with irreversible melting if some ice sheets and a several foot rise in sea levels. They simply cannot pinpoint exactly when that will happen, if it will ever happen. There has never been solid proof of any of the extraordinary predictions made by various global warming groups around the world. (As well as some here in Benicia.)

Some of these extraordinary predictions were made in e-mails just prior to the Copenhagen conference. They were part of a group that was thoroughly debunked by the scientific investigation of a huge amount of professional papers produced by global warming advocates in 2008. Just prior to the Copenhagen conference, they were released before the whole conference fell apart.

Albert Gore, the so-called Guru of Global Warming, packed his bag, cancelled his $3,000 a plate dinner scheduled for 500 of his advocates and flew out of Dodge in his huge Gulfstream 3 private jet. The private plane burns an obscene amount of jet fuel an hour, and is one of two that he owns. He keeps one in this country and one in Europe. At least he did. We don't hear much about Albert lately, just an occasional sighting reported by Willie Brown at the Ritz Carlton where they both reside.

Remarkably, the two decade long climate negotiations have been focused on preventing global temperature from rising no more than 2 degrees above current levels by the end of the century. Folks…that is 88 years from now! And…what they are doing now is trying to get the greenhouse gas emissions to peak before 2020 in order to have a shot at reaching that target. And.,.. they are saying that it is only doable if nations raise their emissions pledges.

Now folks, that is what all of this is about! Money…and little else. The Durban agreement also envisions a new accord with binding targets for all countries to take effect in 2020. And it sets up the "bodies" that will "collect, govern, and redistribute tens of billions of dollars to poor countries suffering the effects of so so called climate change."

Now that little tidbit starts to make things more interesting. "The core now is whether more than1-90 nations can cooperate in order to peak and bring down emissions to the necessary level by 2020 remains open-it is a high risk strategy for the planet and its people", says UNEPO chief Achim Steiner.

There is a bigger question here however. Does any reasonable commonsensical individual actually believe the two biggest carbon polluters, China and the United States, will actually cooperate with that strategy? It is not going to happen folks. Not today or in 2020, or the 88 years after that. Both of these countries are aware that the bulk of those "billions" talked about will be expected from them, and it's not going to happen. It is quite obvious that the money is more important to these organizations than the 2 degrees. Mr. Obama is willing, but not able. He wants to be with us after 2012.

Osama and Obama

The death of Osama bin Laden is currently being credited to the diligence of our current Administration and to President Barack Obama. Obama is wasting no time in taking as much of that credit as he possibly can. It is also true that much of the intelligence that resulted in that shooting in Pakistan was due to the use of "extended methods" (water boarding, etc.) of interrogation by the Central Intelligence Agency during the Bush Presidency.

Although the president has thrown George W. Bush a bone of sorts in the last few days, he has, for the most part, taken most of the credit. I find this very odd given that Obamas's Attorney General is still investigating the CIA agents (for the use of eater boarding and other methods) who obtained most of the information that eventually led to the shooting of Osama in Pakistan.

The president simply can't take credit for something which he declared was obtained illegally just months ago. It was tainted information or it wasn't. In this case, it was legal because it allowed the president to get a huge bump in the polls. This President's moral compass is somewhat out of kilter if he feels that it is alright to do one and the other at the same time. But, if you look at all of this in the long view, you can not help but realize that this president has never backed away from an opportunity to ingratiate himself, regardless of the fact that it sometimes makes him look totally unconcerned about the truth. I have said many times in previous columns that Mr. Obama looks at facts in such a way that they are only represented as he believes them to be, regardless of the truth.

And...if you get your news only from the New York Times, the self-styled newspaper of record, you would have read on Wednesday that information from enhanced interrogations played only a "small role at most" in finding bin Laden. The Times is heavily invested in this story line, having claimed repeatedly over the years that such interrogations are ineffective.

In 2007, former CIA Director Mike Hayden told analysts and operatives at the agency to refocus their search for bin Laden on his courier network. In a radio interview on the afternoon before the Times piece ran, Hayden said that there is a "straight line" between intelligence by interrogators and bin Laden's death.

But it was the comments of the current CIA Director that are particularly newsworthy. Panetta confirmed enhanced interrogation absolutely helped the agency find bin Laden. To some extent then, Barack Obama owes his singular national security achievement to interrogation practices that he condemned for years, and finally banned as president. The confirmation of that deeply ironic point comes from the two most recent heads of the CIA…including the man Obama selected for the job and has now chosen to run the Pentagon.

Governing by Fiat

On April 25 of this year, CNSNEWS.com announced that the National Labor relations Board is seeking a n unprecedented expansion of power in a lawsuit to overturn voter-approved constitutional amendments in at least two states that guarantee the secret ballot for union elections. The NLRB contends that it is perfectly within the agency's jurisdiction to bring a "preemptive" lawsuit against these states.

The agency announced that it would move forward with litigation against the State of South Dakota and to strike the laws from the states that voters approved last November to guarantee employees the right to secret ballot on whether to form unions at their workplace. My home State of South Carolina has a similar amendment to its constitution.

I sincerely believe that someone (anyone?) should inform this rogue agency that the secret ballot is an implied right within the constitutions of these states. It is a clear right, a fundamental right guaranteeing the ballot for a variety of things: for elected officials, for the referendum process and for employment representatives.

This ballot passed in four states by wide margins in November. In Arizona, 61% approved the measure. In South Carolina, 86% of the voters backed the secret ballot, and in South Dakota, 79% approved the amendment and in Utah the initiative was passed with 60% of the vote.

The effort at the state level was in response to the proposed attempt to install a card-check system that would intimidate employees. If you look at historic case law dealing with the NLRB, it typically deals with disputes involving an employee and a business., and it doesn't involve a Federal appointed board. This type of intrusion into the rights of states to run their states in accordance to the wishes of their resident voters is without precedent and, in my opinion, simply out of bounds to any Federal board. The very fact that it has never been attempted before is a fairly good indicator that it is beyond the privy of the NLRB to even attempt to override the wishes of the voters of one state, much less four!

This action by the NLRB is simply political, as Obama and the Democrats could not push card legislative process. The Obama administration was not able to deliver, so it is using National Labor Relations Board as another group of unelected bureaucrats to deliver labor for the presidents' reelection. They look at their mission to partner with big labor unions as a total necessity at this point and will attempt to get that unconditional support in any way available to them. State constitutions be damned.

As a side note: In the first two years of the Obama administration, the head of the SEIU, Andy Stern, was the most frequent visitor to the Oval Office. Now that Mr. Stern has mysteriously retired without explanation, that honor goes to the President of the AFL-CIO. If there is anyone out there who truly believes that this President is not unduly influenced by Labor in this country, then I have this wonderful little Yugo in the garage that I will let you have cheap.

What do we call incompetence these days?

A few days ago, the President of the United States, in a speech to the Congressional Black Caucus, accused those black politicians of being lazy and afraid of the future and not willing to do anything necessary to enhance the programs and illusions of his misguided and misled presidency. It was an all out attack and created no new supporters, that I can assure you.

Nowhere in that speech did Barack Obama accept any blame for the miserable failures of his administration. It was only the members of the Black Caucus that were being castigated. It was only the Black Caucus that was accused of being weak and afraid and lazy. He was angry and terribly disappointed when he said "Throw off your bedroom slippers and get on your hiking boots and go to work" and he showed it for all the world to see!

Not in my memory have I ever heard such rubbish. And for this he was seriously admonished by some members of the Caucus and a surprisingly large element of the press. All of this is just a continuation of the severe downward spiral of this president only 14 months away from the presidential election of 2012.

Nothing seems to be going Mr. Obama's way these days. It all appears to be unraveling before his eyes and the eyes of this nation. He simply refuses to accept any of the responsibility for this. As with the Black Caucus, it has all been the fault of those in his own administration and those nasty guys in the Republican Party, starting with George W. Bush.

But then, on Friday the 30th of September, the president steered the nation's war machine into uncharted territory. For this action, the president has absolutely taken full credit and responsibility. For on that day, a U.S. drone attacked a convoy in Yemen and killed two American citizens who had become central figures in al qaeda.

Today, there are dissenting voices coming out of the woodwork and this has started taking even that satisfaction away from a very troubled presidency. It seems that several libertarian politicians including Ron

Paul, have determined that targeting and killing American citizens, even a turncoat like Anwar al-Awlaki, is against the Constitution of the United States, and thus illegal Can't Barack Obama catch a break once in awhile? The president was well within his powers to order the death of this man, who was clearly a traitor to his country. Can't we just let the anointed one have this little victory and praise him as we did with the death of Osama? Isn't it a shame that the only positive thing this man has done in three years was order the killing of two notorious Muslim leaders in the Middle East?

The truth is: It really has gotten too bad for the president. The victories and the accomplishments have been so few and far between that he has had to desperately grab onto any small positive actions during this three years. No one seems to be supporting his health bill these days, and his Cap and Trade Bill is dead in the water. In reality, this president has nothing positive he can run on between now and November of next year. His far left support is nearly gone because progressives feel he has failed to do the things he promised in 2008, and conservatives and independents just don't believe anything he says any longer. Look for this to be the nastiest presidential election in half a century. The president simply has to go negative, He has no other choice.

Recently, I have observed a swing in that direction, starting with political columnists. A few days ago, Eugene Lyons, a frequent contributor to the Times Herald, actually stated that any white voter not voting for Obama was in reality a racist! Also recently, in the Chronicle, Willie Brown in his Sunday column, said nearly the same thing. I am not surprised that Lyons stated such nonsense, but I am amazed to hear such garbage coming from Brown, a man who is just too smart to be implying such a thing.

It is all simple desperation folks. What else can the supporters of this president do? He cannot run on a record of failure. He has accomplished nearly nothing that he has advocated since becoming president. No faction of his 2008 support is happy with him today. That included a large percentage of the African-American and far left support that appeared to be rock solid during his last campaign. Mr. Obama has clearly shown that one man cannot be everything to every faction at the same time. In this regard, he has clearly failed.

The U.A.W. and Truth

Last month National Review Magazine ran article on the United Auto Workers Union titled The UAW's Last Gamble, in which the authors Vincent Vernuccio and Ian Murray blasted the UAW's no holds barred campaign to organize foreign owned automakers' factories in the United States.

The UAW is in dire straits. By 2009, it had only 355,000 members, down from a high of 1.5 million in 1979. UAW President Bob King has publicly acknowledged the urgency of the union's latest campaign. Speaking to an audience of 1,000 union members recently, he is quoted as stating "If we don't organize these transnationals, I don't think there's a long term future for the United Auto Workers, I really don't.

A labor union doesn't conduct a unionization campaign against a large corporation alone, lest it reveal its self-interested motive in unionizing the corporation. Instead the attack will come from groups allied with the union......including environmental groups, human rights activists, liberal religious groups and self styled consumer advocates. When different groups go after a corporation for seemingly unrelated offenses, from its safety records to its environmental practices, the coordinated nature of the attack remains obscured.

The first and perhaps the most important step in a corporate campaign is for the union to frame the debate. To this end, the UAW has sought to define what makes a union election free and fair. Earlier this year the union released its eleven Principles for Fair Union Elections. As you would expect, the principles stack the deck to favor unionization. The principles include speech restrictions for employers, binding arbitration whereby a third party would write the first contract between an employer and workers, union access to company records, and the potential for card-check organizing.

Card check? Yes. The extremely misnamed Employee Free Choice Act (EFCA) may have died in Congress, but its hugely unpopular card-check provision lives on elsewhere. The UAW's ninth principle, enitled "Secret Ballot" conceded that a secret ballot is "acceptable" but goes on to state that "The parties (i.e. union organizers and management) may select an alternative method on a case by case basis that reflects the best process for demonstrating employee wishes." There is no way to ensure that cards favoring a union have not been obtained by undue pressure or intimidation…practices that the secret ballot was designed to eliminate. And even though our esteemed Congressman George Miller was a strong, strong advocate of the card-check provision, very little was made of it last fall during the election. Miller is owned…lock stock and barrel by labor unions in this state, doubt it? Check it out.

How could an employer agree to such an unfavorable arrangement? That is where the corporate campaign comes in. It stares that the UAW's sixth principle encapsulates the union's strategy. It states that the "UAW will explicitly disavow….messages from community groups that send the message that the company is not operating in a socially responsible way"---but only if management will explicitly disavow…messages from corporate and community groups that send the message that a union would jeopardize jobs". The UAW message is clear: Oppose us and we will use third party groups to demonize you until you agree to a card-check procedure.

The UAW has already hired Jessie Jackson (yes that Jessie) who has years of experience coercing corporations with accusations of racial discrimination (whether real or imagined makes no difference to the man) and threats of bad press or an actual boycott…although not likely, Jessie doesn't have that kind of clout these days. These are the types of attacks that foreign carmakers can expect from the UAW, except that the tribute will not be a simple payoff like Jackson has demanded in the past, but an arrangement to allow the union to organize a company's workers, yielding millions in due for years to come.

Of course, actions taken by the Obama administration have paved the way for the UAW''s use of accusations of human-rights violations as a club.

Last year the Obama White House submitted a self evaluation to the U.N. Human Rights Council. The report said that the extent to which the law facilitates unionization should be a human-rights matter, and the United States fall short in this area.

Folks….there is absolutely no doubt that the UAW was highly instrumental in nearly killing the automobile manufacturing industry in America. Over the last 50 years, the horrendous labor cost to American companies during the construction of automobiles nearly destroyed the industry entirely. Today, both General Motors and Chrysler Corporation are partly owned by the UAW. Due to these labor costs, the quality of materials used in the construction of American automobiles were cheapened to the point that they began to fall apart after only a few years in service.

It was at this point that foreign auto manufacturers began to build their autos in America and in right to work states where membership in a union is not required in order to get a job. This has worked very well for both Honda and Toyota and all the thousands of men and women who build these vehicles. It also means that the cost of these vehicles is lower and as a result the sales price is lower. Both Honda and Toyota have outsold all American manufacturers over the last twenty years., and both brands sold in this country are manufactured here. Anyone who knows well made automobiles knows that these two companies make a fine product and sell them at a fair price. It is the labor unions at the American companies that have nearly destroyed our auto industry.

If the UAW is successful in this attempt to unionize these foreign manufacturers, I have no doubt that both Honda and Toyota will no longer build these models in America. And where does this leave the American public? It leaves us with empty factories and thousands and thousands with out jobs. Given that the Obama administration appears to be actively supporting this attempt at unionizing these plants, one would assume that the White House really doesn't mind this at all. The labor unions in this country have nearly bankrupted this state and many others and this President is bought and paid for by unions including the UAW. When will this stop? We simply, as a nation, cannot continue to go down this road. America is not a union shop. The UAW is under great pressure to get this unionization accomplished before the next election where Mr. Obama is clearly in jeopardy of not being re-elected. If that happens this union is finished as a political power player in America and this country will be better for it.

Following the Osama Aftermath

Now that most of the noise has settled down in the death of Osama bin Laden, policies put in place by this administration that presided over this splendid success, promise fewer such successes in the future. These policies make it unlikely that we'll be able to get information from those whose identities are disclosed by the material seized from bin Laden. The administration also hounds our intelligence gatherers in ways that only demoralize them and...projects our Attorney General as someone who does not necessarily take his order from the President of the United States.

Practices such as waterboarding, in which the suspect's head is covered with water until he believes he is drowning (no one has so far) are used only in extreme cases in which agents know the prisoners have information before the interrogation ever starts. It has always been a last resort attempt to get this information that is desperately needed in most all these vital cases.

The harsh techniques themselves were used very selectively against only a small number of hard core prisoners who successfully resisted all other forms of interrogation, and then only with the explicit authorization of the Director of the CIA. Of the thousands of unlawful combatants captured, fewer than 100 were detained and questioned in the CIA program. According to former Director Michael Hayden, "as late as 2006 even with the growing success of other intelligence tools, fully half of the government's knowledge about the structure and activities of al Qaeda came from those interrogations."

Consider how the intelligence that led to bin Laden came about. It began with a disclosure from Khalid Sheikh Mohammed (KSM) who broke down under the pressure of hard interrogation techniques that included waterboarding. He provided a torrent of information...including eventually the nickname of a trusted bin Laden courier. This information...that led to bin Laden...simply could not have been obtained without this stringent interrogation method.

All of this is old news, as well as the fact that our current Attorney General Eric Holder, is continuing his investigation of the very agents that obtained that information, and treating these men as though they were common criminals. Despite the fact that the bulk of this investigation has been dropped, this man continues to search for any evidence of unusual punishment used during these inquiries. The reasoning behind this behavior is obvious. This Attorney General has never been a willing participant in the search for, or interrogation of, these al Qaeda leaders. In fact, his former New York law firm served as the law firm of record regarding the defense of 14 of these terrorists being held in Cuba at this time.

Is it me... or doesn't Holder get his marching orders from the president? Had we been prevented from using these extreme methods of interrogation, we would not have found and eliminated Osama bin Laden. If this president did not want Holder to continue his ongoing investigation of the very men who obtained the information that resulted in that action, do you think for a minute he would be continuing till this day doing that which the President did not agree with?

It is impossible not to associate Mr. Obama with the actions of his Attorney General. Of course! Holder gets his marching orders from the president. Do you think that Mr. Obama could not order that investigation closed should he desire to do so? The fact is...Mr. Obama is between a rock and a hard place. With his far left support falling day by day, he must maintain some semblance of an ultra leftwing program. In the meantime, these fine men are forced to suffer the shame of a public investigation. That makes them look like the "Bad Guys". These actions of Holder and Obama are out there for all to see, and where is the press during all of this? Where they always are, supporting and promoting a president that doesn't seem to know who the real "Bad Guys" are himself. Perhaps we might start taking a longer look at the media, it appears to contain all the necessary criteria to define the term.

South of the Border

What has been happening on our border with Mexico in the last few years is beyond comprehension. And...this is not entirely an Obama thing (Bush had his hand in this debacle also). In his near desperation to secure the Hispanic vote in 2012, Mr. Obama has refused to do ANYTHING to help the Governors of Texas, California, but most grievously Arizona, to cope with a deluge of illegal crossing their borders.

This has become a desperate situation in Arizona and is headed that way at this time in Texas and California. We have in Washington, a Secretary of Homeland Security who regularly downplays the debacle on our Southern Border. This woman, Janet Napolitano, is so tone deaf to this situation that these governors, (exempting Jerry Brown), have started to take desperate actions to force the Obama administration to provide them help in stopping this flood of illegals before these people bankrupt their states.

We have in Washington a culture dedicated to provide another homeland for Spanish speaking peoples in the Western Hemisphere. Residing in the West Wing of the White House, we have a large group of so called "experts" on Latin affairs that declare that we are compelled to help these people on humanitarian grounds. These illegals are not, mind you, starving or afraid for their lives. These are people that are simply looking to "do better" in providing for their families. In order to provide this opportunity, the Obama administration is willing to place on the Border States a burden that they simply cannot bear. Due to a terrible economy and the burden of 3 wars, this country simply is not capable of taking in 12-15 million additional citizens who are without a means to support themselves. It is imply not viable. Now...this may sound harsh, but this administration is not doing this out of the goodness of their hearts, they are doing this in order to create a huge new voting source dedicated to this President and the Democratic Party. They continually deny that is the motive, but facts are the facts! And...the fact is, Mr. Obama has steadfastly avoided these states and he and his party have steadily refused to help these border governors to cope with this travesty.

I would appear that the Obama administration has simply written off the possibility of carrying these states in 2012. They should. If the president continues (without explanation) to refuse them additional troops and border patrol agents, we are going to see some terrible things happen on these borders. And they are happening right now…and every day.

Now let me ask you…my readers…a simple question. Where is the Mainstream Media in all of this? Why is Press secretary Carney not being deluged with questions regarding the failure of this administration to solve at least some of these problems? Why at times do weeks go by without one of these clowns even mentioning the Southern Border and the huge problems there? There are greater problems elsewhere they say. The president has bigger fish to fry they say. The governors can do more to help themselves they say. What on this green world has happened to journalism in America?

Why has not some enterprising reporter had the gumption to ask Mr. Carney why the President has continuously avoided meeting with Governor Perry of Texas and the Governor of Arizona? Do you think that Mr. Obama is convinced that Janet Napolitano is absolutely correct when she tells the Governor of Arizona that her border with Mexico is perfectly safe and stronger than ever? Do you think that the President is convinced that Napolitano is better informed than the Governor of the State of Arizona? Well….the White House press corps certainly appears to believe that! Or they are simply too intimidated to say otherwise. As an instrument of the people to control the executive branch of this government, this press corps is made up of a large group of deaf and dumb eunuchs.

Just today, the Governor of New York announced that he would no longer work with Federal authorities in regard to illegal immigration. Our own Jerry Brown is also making noises about doing the same. As far as I am aware, this is the first peep out of Jerry regarding anything to do with immigration. Mr. Brown, who was the recipient of nearly 80% of the

Hispanic vote in this state in the last election, is finally making the right sort of stand on immigration.

I am somewhat surprised that Brown, (who has hinted that he may not run for a second term) has not taken a firmer stance previously. Actually, if a second term is out, then he would be free to do something without political consideration. WOW wouldn't that be something to see? In this case….it would be going out doing the right thing.

Were we really paying any attention?

On the 19th of May, our president demanded in a televised speech that Israel retreat from it current borders to the lines set in 1967. This came as a shock to even his staff and surely to the Nation of Israel. It makes one wonder why Mr. Obama would want to bring Israel back to 7 miles wide at its narrowest point. In this configuration, it would lose the Jordan Valley and would be incapable of defending itself against Arab invasion.

The fact is: Mr. Obama has absolutely no authority to demand such a thing. This "suggestion" as he now calls it (after a torrent of criticism from leaders around the world, including England, Germany, and France) had, according to staff members not even been mentioned around the West Wing recently. This begs the question: Who is advising this president in regard to foreign affairs? I find it difficult to imagine that Secretary of State Hillary Clinton had even thought of something as radical as this. The West Wing is, however, so full of strange political thought (that is putting it mildly) that it is definitely possible that such an idea could have originated there, and probably did. This group of radicals are decidedly anti-Israel.

Barack Obama has made it clear from the inception of this presidency that he has a special regard for Palestinian causes and quite a bit less for Israel. His speech in Cairo less than a month after being sworn in as president, indicated that he was a very close friend of Muslim causes in the Middle East. This should have sent a signal to Israel, and it did. Yet at no time has he tried to mollify the uneasiness of the Israel government and has even gone so far as to humiliate and insult Prime Minister Netanyahu on several occasions recently.

I find it strange that this president could treat the leader of our closest ally in the Middle East in such an obscene manner. But…he did and he received very little flack from it by the American press. It is very obvious that his president is basically disregarding the massive monetary support that Democrat presidents have received over the years. Although he must be aware of the 75 million dollars that he received in 2008 from Jewish organizations in this country, and that does not include huge additional contributions from very wealthy Jewish individuals in this country and world wide. The combined total of those contributions was much larger than was attributed to George Soros and his minions in this country and abroad.

In addition, a great number of Christian Church organizations in America feel very close to the nation of Israel and would be expected to be a large loss should they withdraw their monetary support to the Obama campaign. Could someone please explain to me what prompted this man to make this unilateral move against the Jewish state that only makes a tense situation ever more tense? What good does it serve the U.S. to support a man who has a clear intent to further intimidate and humiliate the Prime Minister of Israel and…in doing so, create an even more negative atmosphere in the entire region?

The actions of Barack Obama do not coincide with his flowery rhetoric regarding his intentions in the Middle East. My God! Does he believer the electorate in this country, as well as people around the world, can not see what he is doing? It is glaring in its simplicity and frankly arrogant in it purpose. But… arrogance is a word that is becoming more and more associated with this president.

Solyndra LLC (Show Me the Money)

Today (0/1/2011), Solyndra LLC of Femont announced that the solar panel manufacturer was laying off 1100 workers and filing Chapter11 Bankruptcy.

For those who are unfamiliar with the firm, Solyndra was at one time the poster child for government investments in Green Technology. In May 2010, the President visited the plant along with Arnold Schwarzenegger and the Secretary of Energy Steven Chiu.

This was big time, folks. The Government, as part of the stimulus, had given Solyndra $ 535,000,000 in stimulus money in addition to over one billion dollars they had received in private investments. In a little over 15 months since that visit, all of that money is gone and the fingers are pointing everywhere.

Sometimes I get the feeling that most people just don't realize how much money one and a half **billion** dollars is. Trust me, it is one heck of a lot of money! So where is the money today? That is not an unreasonable question, but it appears to be a little too involved for Solyndra to come up with a quick answer. Simply put, the executives at Solyndra just don't know. There is that $733,000,000 physical plant and way too much inventory, but that appears to be just about it.

It seems to be a real mystery, do you or anyone else know? Evidently not. Somehow half of that huge amount of money, both government and privately provided, has simply disappeared. I have not had the time nor the opportunity to research this matter in any way. But the simple fact is: Solyndra is broke. It appears that the competition (primarily China) has underbid the Fremont corporation and taken all the business.

China can produce the solar panels (the primary product of Solyndra) for a whole lot less money and then, of course, sell them for a whole less money!

This is not just a Solyndra problem. Two other solar panel manufacturers in this country have gone under within the last two weeks. Is it me, or is somebody simply missing the point here? To produce and sell a product at a profit, a corporation must understand its competition and its own ability to price a product in a manner that will provide a profit. Evidently, Solydra was not alone in its ability to compete with China. The other two corporations producing panels were no more successful against the Chinese. Surely, all of these American manufacturers were aware of the Chinese pricing structures before they began to produce their product.

And yet, Solyndra found the means to acquire a huge amount of public and private money before they ever produced a product. And they produced very little of it. And...now they will never produce any more of it. Does that make any more sense to you than it does to me? If it does, do you think you might find it in your heart to fill me in?

Another point that has not been examined here is the fact that the product itself is simply not in great demand in this country. No matter how hard certain companies and other entities have tried to sell solar energy as the savior of American industry (some right here in Benicia), they have failed to convince corporate board rooms. Solar energy at this time has not been proven to be any better than normal energy sources and it costs much more money to produce. Looking at this, it is no wonder that these three solar energy manufacturers have failed in the last three weeks.

According to WIKIPIDIA, there are six manufacturers who produce solar panels that are more efficient than the Solyndra product. They include German, Taiwanese, and Chinese firms. On March 20, 2009, the US Department of Energy offered a $535 million loan guarantee to Solyndra LLC to support the construction of a commercial scale manufacturing plant for its proprietary solar photovoltaic panels. Think about that for a minute. Even though they were aware that Solyndra was far behind its basic competition, they still offered the company nearly a half a **billion** dollars in loan guarantees.

On March 2009, Solyndra estimated to the Government and its prospective investors:

- The construction of its complex would employ approximately 3,000 people

- The operation of the facility would create over 1,000 jobs in the United States
- The installation of these panels would create hundred of additional jobs in the United States
- The commercialization of this technology was expected to then be duplicated in multiple other manufacturing facilities.

Yet, in November 2010, Solyndra said it would lay off around 40 employees and not renew contracts for about 150 temporary workers as a result of consolidation.

And …on August 31, 2011, Solyndra announced it was filing for Chapter 11 Bankruptcy protection, laying off 1100 employees, and shutting down all operations and manufacturing.

Think about the time element here. From March 2009 to August 2022 (30 months), Solyndra went from startup to bankrupt and between the government and private investment, lost **one billion five hundred million dollars**. Now that is mouth full isn't it?

There has to be some sort of practical business education here, but for the life of me, I can't figure out what it is. The investors should have darn well known better. But that is their problem, and why should anyone care any way? But that $535,000,000 belonged to you and me, and…we should absolutely care.

As long as there is this insistent drive to prove "Green Energy" to be the only way to go, we will continue to be caught up in this "anything green is better" pathology. And folks…it can be very, very expensive, as well as addictive. Think about that when the word "sustainability" pops up. Right now, there are a lot of people trying to figure out just where that other $700,000 went to. Given that we are still looking to find most of the stimulus money, the percentages are pretty slim, wouldn't you think?

Time Out

Recently it has occurred to me that we as a country have reached a point in our history when we have simply lost the ability to recognize a con when we see it. Never before have we been totally unable to see the outright subterfuge of politics in America. I am not speaking of any particular party for absolutely one is nearly as bad as another.

The very fact that we are being led by a president that is the most under qualified supreme commander this nation has ever known, is proof of the ability of the major media in this country to pull off the perfect long con on the American public. Had anyone in January 2007 announced that out next president would be a Freshman Senator from Chicago without an ounce of diplomatic or executive experience, it would have generated hilarious laughter with in the political press corp. But…that is what we got folks…that is what we got.

Disregarding our current leadership, this nation is in a serious mess. We disparage our allies and praise our sworn enemies. We insult and humiliate our closest ally in the Middle East while we try to ignore those that are trying diligently to put a knife in our back. Pakistan is a prime example of the mess we have created and it just might be the most critical area in the world at this time. We have been paying Pakistan over 2 billion dollars a year to be our friend in that part of the world and guess what? They aren't. The average Pakistani despises this country and looks upon Afghanistan as their brother nation. Our diplomacy in that part of the world is so inept as to make one wonder if we have a comedy team writing the script.

Hillary Clinton is an intelligent woman but she is not a diplomat. A woman representing this nation diplomatically in a part of the world where women are not even allowed to drive a car or vote, makes no sense at all. In addition, it is doubtful that Clinton had she been a strong Secretary of State, would have been given clear authority to set an example in Egypt and Libya. So…we have a president without any diplomatic experience running the State Department himself. If you were curious about why George Mitchell resigned his position as the Presidential Representative in the Middle East, cease to wonder. This president does not listen to advice that differs with his own opinions. Thus we have a huge debacle going on all over that region. And…it is not likely to get any better under our current leadership.

Given all of this, it would be reasonable to assume that our major news networks would be thoroughly advised of the inability of our current administration to do a thing about it. They aren't…or if they are, they aren't willing to tell the people of this nation about it.

I know that I have been severely attacked by the progressives in the area in regard to my willingness to call out Mr. Obama on his constant inability to get on top of any international crisis, but he is not getting the job done. I care not about his political party, or his arrogance. I care about his inability to run this country in a time of crisis. And even moiré than that, I despise a media that refused to expose what a mess he has made of this country in a little over two years. The media may not tell you, but I will as long as I am allowed to.

Civil Liberties....Really?

Recently, I read an article by a local writer extolling the wonderful attributes of the American Civil Liberties Union (ACLU). No where in that article did the author mention the attempt by the ACLU to end all drone aircraft attacks against al Qaeda in Pakistan and other locations throughout the Middle East. But that information has finally reached the major media in this country. No small feat that. al Qaeda, should you not be aware is the same organization that planned and carried out the attacks of 9/11/2000 on the cities of New York and Washington.

The very idea that an American organization made up of actual Americans of sane(?) mind, with American mothers and fathers, would actually defend and support these terrorists rather than the men of the military, staggers the imagination.

The first inclination is to label these people as a bunch of crazies, albeit dangerous crazies, and a bunch that should have their passports lifted and shown to the door, and for keeps. There is just no plausible explanation for this seditionist attempt to undermine our government----in some parts of the world—it would be called treason.

The American Civil Liberties Union has sued the Federal Government to learn the use of unmanned drones for targeted killings by the military, and in particular, the C.I.A. The law suit asks for information on when, where, and against whom drone attacks can be authorized; the number and rate of civilian casualties and other information essential for assessing the wisdom and legality of using armed drones to conduct target killings.

I must confess that I just don't understand the mine set of these people. But then, I don't have to understand this bunch to totally detest them all. The remarkable part of all this is the free pass this group gets by the mainstream media in America. I have lobbied them all (the ACLU, the media, and the Administration) together into one despicable brotherhood. This works very well for me. Somehow there is something total NOT American about this group. Even the name of this organization is a misnomer

The very strongest supporter of the ACLU in Washington, (exempting the President) is the Attorney General of the United States, Eric Holder. He and his former New York City law firm, in conjunction with the ACLU, have defended over 30 of these al Qaeda terrorists over the last ten years and several of these same lawyers are now working for the Justice Department headed by Holder.

In the last year Holder has attempted to move the terrorist trials from Cuba to New York City. This, to my mind, is indefensible, and Holder is a disgrace to the office, but no more guilty of gross miscalculations than his boss---who has given him the green light—and then withdrawn his backing. At this point, we don't know where they will hold these trials, if they hold them at all.

The ACLU has long been one of the most controversial organizations in the country, and it has never been shy about its left-wing-Socialist bend. It has also never been shy about support from some rather shady sources such as the American Communist Party. In addition, liberal lawyers, particularly graduates of prominent East Coast law schools such as Columbia, Yale, and Harvard have long provided large amounts of monetary and moral support, and pro-bono legal representation. As well…the mainstream media in this country has been shamefully defending and hiding the ACLU's bad behavior regardless of just how seditious and totally without merit some of these law suits have been.

In return, the ACLU has supported and provided legal assistance to some of the most outrageous and controversial legal stands in the history of jurisprudence in this country. The ACLU has always looked down its' nose at the "common" law of America. Instead, it has specialized in supporting various groups and organizations that represent the dregs of all segments or our society. In addition, it has always preferred to represent clients who, for the most part, stood for clearly anti-American and anti- religious causes. In fact, it appears that they are more than a little proud of those anti-American positions.

The pendng law suit against the United States by the ACLU in regard to attacks on al Qaeda bases and leaders, has no standing and simply no chance of prevailing at this time. Despite the huge number of proud leftist judges in America, this one should not succeed. Not now or ever. The parade of politically correct leftist causes will have to find another champion. And perhaps the ACLU should be looking for a first class attorney to represent their own organization. They just might be needing one.

According to Jameel Jaffer, Director of Policy of the ACLY National Security Project, "These kinds of questions ought to be discussed and debated publicly, not resolved secretly behind closed doors. While the Obama Administration may legitimately withhold intelligence information as well as sensitive information about military strategy, it should disclose basic information about the scope of the drone program, the legal basis for the program, and the civilian casualties that have resulted from the program.

The simply astounding actions of this leftist organization, particularly its recent lawsuit against the United States in regard to those drone attacks, leaves any intelligent, patriotic American with no other choice than to insist on a complete investigation of the entire group. I cannot understand how George Miller or any ther member of Congress could possibly decline to do so. This organization (ACLU) has the support of nearly every leftist group in the country who themselves have the support of every leftist overlord in the country, such as George Soros and a bevy of Hollywood light weights like Alec Baldwin and George Clooney whose combined intelligence quotient might reach 95.

Elena Kagan Revisited

In May of last year, I wrote an in-depth appraisal of new Supreme Court justice Elena Kagan, in which I said "her involvement in many legal cases as Barack Obama's Solicitor General are going to be a problem for her in the future." That time has come, as dozens of GOP members of the U.S. House apparently agree.

Th failure of Ms. Kagan to recuse herself from judging cases challenging the President's Healthcare Law has become a serious legal issue, and rumblings of an official investigation are on the horizon amid doubts about the veracity of her answers to the Senate Judiciary Committee during her confirmation.

From the beginning, Ms. Kagan's confirmation testimony raised serious questions. There may well have been a conflict of intentions: The intent of the majority of the committee was to get Ms. Kagan confirmed, regardless of the manner by which that confirmation was obtained. Evidence shows that she was coached to provide answers satisfactory to Republican members of the committee.

Given that Democrats were in the majority on the committee and there was nearly no chance of her not being confirmed, I am puzzled as to the reasoning behind the subterfuge. But this sort of under-the-table atmosphere has permeated everything in this Administration. Constant misdirection, obfuscation and counterfactual posturing have been the hallmarks of Obamas's term in office, even when transparency and openness would be more practical. This President has been a stranger to the truth from the first day of his campaign in 2008.

Now 49 members of the House have demanded a probe into Ms. Kagan's involvement in formulating the Healthcare Law when she was Solicitor General. Personally, I find any such investigation to be a huge waste of time. What do the Republicans think they are going to do, succeed in the removal of Ms. Kagan from the high court? Not likely, my friends. To my knowledge, this has never been accomplished.

In any case, hearings on the matter appear to be of no practical use to anyone. Ms. Kagan is on that Court and she will die there or retire of her own volition, regardless of the fact that she is the worst nominee since G.W. Bush tapped Harriet Miers.

The Republican Party needs to be more diligent in stopping the confirmation of candidates they are convinced are not fit for the Court. If they can't achieve that, then they must find some way to set the bar higher and require much stiffer investigations of all candidates. Over the years, Democratic Presidents have been much more successful in getting their appointees approved---and there is a reason for that.

Simply put, Conservatives view the left as a bunch of wild-eyed utopians beholden to harebrained schemes and fantasies that can work only in the imagination of some quirky sociology or law professor with too much time on his hands. But in the debate in the courts-the Elena Kagan nomination being a prime example,-it is Conservatives who become the wild-eyed utopians and the Liberals who operate as the realists.

The left long ago recognized that courts are political institutions that can be used to further apolitical agenda. The right, in contrast, long refused to accept the inevitable and is only recently coming around to this fact.

Failing to recognize that the courts long ago became politicized, Conservatives embrace flawed notions such as judicial restraint and strict constructionism, demanding a return to a world in which courts play a limited role in American government and politics. But that is pure fantasy. We can never go back to that world.

Sure, it would be lovely if courts didn't practice judicial activism, but we must accept the courts as they are: political institutions with extraordinary power to invent rights not mentioned in the Constitution; to overturn democratically enacted laws; and, as well as change, laws.

Like it or not, judicial activism is with use to stay. Advocating judicial restraint now, given the current State of Arizona law and legal culture, is akin to trying to fight a modern war with 17th century weapons. Allowing the left to pillage our cities with the weapons of judicial activism while we stand throwing the flowers of judicial restraint in their way is a path to dismal failure.

For the Republican Party, a new tactic is required. The GOP will have to do a heck of a lot more than hold hearings over an already seated Supreme Court Justice if they hope to change the way these proceedings have taken place, now or in the future. That fight has been fought: it's time to look ahead to the next one, and the one after that

The Party would be much betterserved if its members, and its base, concentrated more on removing the man who placed Ms. Kagan on the high court. Of the two of them, Mr. Obama is much more dangerous to this country.

Like all real Conservatives, I pride myself on being a hardened political realist—on being rational, knowing history, understanding economics and human nature, and looking at the world as it really is., not as I would like it to be. We, as a nation, have a mountain of problems whose importance require attention, and these dwarf Ms. Kagan's status on the Supreme Court. That is where our Representatives need to concentrate their efforts, today and in the future.

Obama and the U. N.

Recently, both Jewish American and Christian supporters of Israel have become alarmed by a United Nations speech given by President Obama in which Obama coupled supporting Israel security with Israel fulfilling Palestinian claims and rights. According to Gordon Klein, president of the Zionist Organization of America, "He could have said, I support Israel security, and I want Israel to fulfill Palestinian claims and rights. But, he didn't say that. He used the word couple-linking it."

That linkage has never been made by any president ever. According to Klein, "That was an astonishingly new statement. That really frightens both Christian and Jewish American supporters of Israel." In addition, in a speech in Cairo he never mentioned Iran at all, and appears to be doing everything he can to delay any real, true sanctions and seems to have taken the military option off the table.

All of this is making the State of Israel very nervous and is doing absolutely nothing to strengthen the American and Israel relationship in the Middle East. This attitude toward Israel is doing nothing but encouraging the little hate monger in Iran to think that he is in a stronger position than he really is. A miscalculation on his part could lead to an attack by Israel on Iranian nuclear facilities and it could come sooner than you might think.

This is a very dangerous business. It is scary business, and it boggles the mind to think that Obama is not aware of it. Frankly, I believe he is very aware of what he is doing. What I don't know is why he is doing it. There is some political thought out there that believes that deep down, his childhood Muslim training has influenced him to the extent that he feels almost obligated to support the downtrodden Palestinian cause. I don't get the feeling that he has much love for Israel at all.

There are many among the far left in America that feel Israel has assumed for far too long that America is obligated to come to its rescue if it is threatened. These people are wrong. This country is obligated not only to Israel but to the whole Middle East to remain as the referee. This part of the world desperately needs "big daddy" to step in and spank the "bad boys" when they are naughty. Without Israel at our back, "big daddy" loses an awful lot of his clout in that part of the world.

In the meanwhile, Klein believes that Obama "may have become the most hostile president to Israel ever". He believes that Obama's sympathies and feelings are not that far from his mentor Rev. Jeremiah Wright. All of this makes you wonder if the president realizes just how much sympathy and support Israel has in this country. Does he have any idea about the massive political clout that Jewish organizations like the Zionist Organization of America have in this country? Evidently not, but if it were to ever come to a showdown between the Obama Whit House and the Jewish support in America, well...the president might as well start looking for a new job right now.

Obama's Failure to Perform

On March 20, 2011, the Benicia Herald ran a column by Creators Syndicate Writers' columnist Mona Charen which highlighted the consistent disrespect President Obama has shown to the State of Israel since he has taken office.

Toward the end of the summer last year, I wrote a similar column here in the Herald in which I said basically the same thing but with more detail and a harder edge. The total disrespect shown to Israeli Prime Minister Benjamin Netanyahu after the Prime Minister had announced the building of 1,600 new apartments in Jerusalem, was a slap in the face of the Nation of Israel. And it was unfortunately led by our Vice President and Secretary of State.

Ms. Caren is absolutely correct when she decries the horror knife killing of an entire Jewish family on the West Bank as reprisal for daring to construct those buildings. Her admonition of that massacre was not shared by our President, however. As Charen stated, there was "no ongoing campaign to shame or humiliate the Palestinians. No list of action that were to be undertaken to show their good faith revulsion".

"This family was not just killed by two men, they were the victims of the death cult that Palestinian society has bred".

And neither Vice President Joe Biden (who claimed to have been blindsided by the announcement of the construction) or Hilary Clinton (who delivered a blazing 45 minute harangue about Israel's decision to build the apartments) appeared to be willing to condemn any Muslim faction for the killings. This administration, from it's inception, has taken a clearly negative stance against Israel and continues to do so.

The treatment of the Prime Minister during a White House visit following that episode last year, was so extraordinarily obnoxious as to bring shame upon the office of this president. And yet there has been no apology from the White House. Realistically, there is not likely to ever be one.

Folks, what we have here is a President of the United States that has insulted, embarrassed and humiliated the Prime Minister of our closest ally in the Middle East, and at the same time embarrassed himself and his country. This is the man who claims he has never shown bias approval of Mahmound Abbas (Palestinian Authority) and laughs at being accused of being Muslim. Yet…he leaves the Prime Minister of Israel in a White House room unattended (without so much as a glass of water) for more than an hour while he has dinner, and does this without an apology.

In addition, we have a President who cuts and runs every time he has to confront a situation in which he feels uncomfortable, and in which he is obviously not experienced enough to handle. He has done this over and over during the last two years.

Why on earth was it necessary for the President to fly off to Brazil while there was a very current crisis going on in Lybia, Egypt and Japan? The Press in this country continues to ignore the non-action of this man who continues to do nothing. Might not this suggest to the rest of the world that to him it is not so important? There is something very odd going on here. Mr. Obama simply appears not to know what to do (can you say Lybia?), and he is not closely surrounded by anyone else that does. He has from the time he took office appointed only individuals that he felt were not his equal (his ego is enormous) who offer only opinions they feel he will approve of or that are not likely to interfere with his decision on anything. As a result, he now has no one with enough experience and common sense to turn to for real help and advice. Just look at his Cabinet and tell me I am wrong.

Thus he is surrounded by a bunch of not so smart 'yes men'. And that might work for him, but it can quickly turn into a disaster for this country. How long is it going to take the Press to wake up and show this man for what he really is….an inexperienced ideologist. He is not a competent, experienced, international leader, he never has been. This absolutely is not a good thing for America or for the rest of the world. November 20212 seems far- far away. We need a strong President now!

No Coming Back

According to a recent National Review: "For the last half century, Bartack Obama has simply had to be. Just being Obama was enough to waft him onwards and upwards: He was the head of the Harvard Law Review who never published a word, the community organizer who never organized a thing, the state legislator who voted present. And then one day came the time when it wasn't enough simply to be. For the first time in his life, he had to do…And healthcare.com is about what you would expect if you nationalized a sixth of the economy and gave it to the Assistant Deputy Commissar of the Department of Paperwork and the Under-Regulator-General of the Bureau of Compliance.

No thoughtful American could possibly be a fan of the railroaded Obamacare Bill, crafted like Frankenstein's monster by House Minority Leader Nancy Pelosi in her quivering moment of glory. Launched against her own countrymen in the dead of night and wrapped in the haughty regalia of self-proclaimed ignorance (and with the compassion of a nest of cobras). Mrs. Pelosi and her accomplices stuffed a societal death sentence down America's throat.

History will indeed record this act as the signature of a president who succeeded in transforming America from the evil empire he seemingly imagined it to be into something else nearly as repulsive. President Obama has attempted to take us from the "exemplar of freedom" throughout the world to a sniveling nanny state in which there are no superlatives or true morality and no urge for individual achievement. Isn't it profoundly sad that we have allowed this to happen on our watch? Mr. Obama and his confederates have succeeded in plowing us toward the most Pyrrhic of victories. It was to be his crowning achievement. But…bad things happened.

Indeed, the old GOP guard is inept and has lost both its understanding of the central themes of our republic and its will to join the battle for

American survival. Yet, there are a few Patrick Henrys still left out there. Other would-be patriots are in hiding, still rationalizing. They would have never stood on Bunker Hill. Yet, what were "we the people" to do? The answer was simple: ignore the main stream media, which has (unfortunately) become nothing more today than a facto agent of the Obama administration. And…we must learn (among other things) to live within our means. Horrendous national debt is a critical national problem folks. No matter what Mr. Obama says or thinks.

There actually are brave and vocal folks on Capital Hill today who still know that even with all the Obama deferrals and exemptions and chicanery designed to produce faux benefits in order to inveigle higher –ups, Obamacare has crashed and is burning at this very moment. No American president at this point in his presidency has ever fallen to this extent in the polls and made a full comeback. That is a fact folks, and I welcome you to try to prove me wrong.

Whether you like it or not

According to a recent issue of *Foreign Policy Magazine, "Forget Russia, these days it's Barrack Obama who is the proverbial riddle wrapped in a mystery, inside an enigma". In regard to government controlled and operated healthcare in this country, no one has ever managed to present more confusion and elevated ill feelings more than our President. And even a man of unmatched speaking ability such as Mr. Obama is lost when trying to navigate in the fog of this dilemma.*

Make no mistake, I am not attempting to present Mr. Obama in any way other than a man dedicated to his dream of all Americans acquiring proper healthcare. That part is easy…everything else is so murky it is hard providing 30 million people in this country coverage they currently do not have, without raiding taxes on all of the rest of us, is a question he or anyone else, seems to be able to answer.

Actually, the answer is fairly simple…there is no answer! We don't have the ability to provide the kind of money necessary to make that possible without borrowing more money from China. And yet, the President and the Democratic Party keep coming at us ad nausea with plan after plan that the people of this country simply don't want. It seems to make no difference to this man that this country lacks the financial credibility and the moral necessity to shove this thing through…come hell or high water.

For 14 months, Obama in front of the cameras, in front of the microphones, talking up his health plan. Today he says that "it appears that I simply have not explained my plan properly". Yes you have Mr, President, you have explained it again and again. We know what it is and we don't want it and cannot afford it. Enough already Sir!

Today the president gave us a 20 minute speech in which He announced his version of Obamacare. It included a half dozen Republican suggestions, but little else that was any different from what we have been fed for over a year.

What was different was his announcement that he was going to push his bill through using an up and down vote! In other words, he was going to use the 51 vote "nuclear option" or "reconciliation".

By doing this he is telling the majority for his country (73%) that he was going to pass that bill (whether we like it or not). Such arrogance by a president has never been seen in this country before now. He said in that short speech that he was not concerned about the politics of that thing...really? He explained that people need it and he was going to give it to them healthcare (some version), and let the chips fall; where they may.

I am hard pressed not to look at that performance as anything other than high political drama directed at a small minority or radicals with an agenda not friendly to the majority of American voters. It makes no sense whatever to do this the way he is doing it. The urgency is simply not there. The men and women who vote to pass this bill will, no doubt, be falling on their own swords. The question we are left with it this: Why are they doing it? I there something in the water in Washington that is causing temporary insanity? Obama has stated that it matters not to him that he may be a one term president. That could surely come to pass, but why he is taking 51 additional politicians with him can only be guessed at.

Total Waste of Money

Today on 11 /1/2011, I am sitting at the desk in my study contemplating just what would be the best method in which to arouse my friends and neighbors here in Benicia in regard to just how extremely important these next eleven months are going to be to each and every one of us. It is extremely critical that we understand that America is under siege from enemies within and without.

The international status of this country has fallen significantly under this President during the last eighteen months. Simply put, other nations around the globe no longer look upon this country as the leader of the civilized world. Countries in the Middle East, including Pakistan, a nation that we have provided huge amounts of support, (both military and financial over the last ten years), no longer respect or fear the United States.

Afghanistan has been the recipient of billions of American dollars since 2001. This money has been directed to Afghanistan in spite of the anti-American attitude and actions of the asinine leadership in that country. The fact is, the Afghanistan government, for the most part, despises the United States. Always has and always will continue to do so as long as we have a military presence on the ground there. This Afghan president (Karzai) has managed to hide away hundreds of millions of dollars in European banks over this period and can be expected to fly away to collect it the moment we decide to saddle up and get out of Dodge.

All over the globe America has become the "Great Satan" of the Muslim religion. Barack Obama has done everything he could do to

Obama: 2012 The Fourth Year

During the year 2012 it became very clear to the American public that we were dealing with a president that was obviously incapable of coping with the responsibilities of the office without a great deal of assistance and advice…which he was not willing to receive.

It has been very difficult to write a political column about national politics during the first three and a half years without discussing the negative aspects of this president. It simply cannot be denied that Barack Obama has been one of, if not the most, incompetent presidents this nation has ever had to endure.

It is difficult for any president to promise everything to everyone and not disappoint most. And that is what this man has done during his first campaign and continuing to this day. It simply cannot be done and even as inexperience as Mr. Obama was when elected, he certainly should have known that.

Book Titles 2012

2012 Obama Time

Climate Change and the Chronicle

Fundraiser Supreme

Craig Becker and the NLRB- 2012

A Job for a Mental Therapist

What do you know about the 10th Amendment

What Wisconsin Predicts

A Serious Problem in America

Inequality in America

Obama and the French

Our "Constitutional" Lawyer /President

A Practiced Form of Deceit

Never Let a Good Crisis Go to Waste

Goodwin Liu Revisited

Come Hell or High Water

Obama Time

On this day, January 8, 2012, the President of the United States is in the process of taking his public political perception hard right. This move was anything but unexpected. President Clinton had done precisely that at the turn of his first term.

The causes of this action were very similar in that both had suffered rather humiliating defeats during their first midterm elections. The surprising part of this, however, was the fact that Barack Obama has moved right in less than half the time of Clinton and more resolve.

There are many opinions regarding just what makes this president tick politically. I am, as are many other political writers, taking a fresh look at this man at this time. I do not deny that I have felt strongly that Barack Obama is an ideologue incapable of making pragmatic decisions but, I may be wrong.

There is no doubt that he hasn't Clinton's political savvy, but the political moves he has made since November 2, have a very familiar Clinton look about them. One thing that is regularly overlooked, however, is the fact that his staff is loaded with former Clinton staffers. The president may have tipped his hand when he called in Clinton to support his position during a press conference on the tax cut extension. Clinton took over the show and was a big hit. The big move to the center followed swiftly. Obama may not have Clinton's savvy, but he is improving.

Frankly, if he makes a Clinton like change and it is good for this country, I am all for it. If he continues to make smart political decisions that benefit America for the next 2 years, then he will deserve a re-election. I sincerely hope he does, and even if I personally distrust the gentleman, I can live with that.

But folks…it ain't going to happen. This leopard simply can't change that many spots. The president spends just too much time in shadowy covert alleys where sneaky moves are the order of the day and the players who live there don't show up as cuddly characters like the cast of a new SHREIK sequel.

And isn't that what this is all about? Do you actually have a clue about the number of recorded unfulfilled promises this man has made since he started to campaign in 2008? Well, let me tell you. It is 38. It is like he just winged it folks! It was like "Won't they love this one"! The people did love them…they also remembered them. Uh oh! Did Barack actually believe they wouldn't?

And even though it was 38 basic lies, (what else can you call them?) the mainstream Press in this country ignored them completely. Well… it is the same President isn't it? But fortunately for us, it is not the same Press. Somewhere along the line, something woke these people up. Barack Obama can not win another term in the White House with empty promises and a broad smile.

The odds of re-election in 2012 for Mr. Obama are not encouraging for the Democarat Party, but it is not impossible. If the president realizes that trust is the key to his election chances and starts to actually be honest with Electorate, then he has a shot. But, politicians, like poker players have a "tell" when they are bluffing. With our President the "tell" is his lips are moving and when his lips are moving…well you know.

Climate Change and the Chronicle

Early in June of this year, the San Francisco Chronicle ran an article titled "Close to tipping point of warming". The article consisted of little more than 100 words above the fold on the front page, and ended with 12 very short paragraphs on page A 14.

According to this article, written by Chronicle Science Editor David Perlman, "the Earth is reaching a "tipping point" in climate change that will lead to increasingly rapid and irreversible destruction of the global environment unless its forces are controlled by concerted international action. Unchecked population growth, the disappearance of critical plant and animal species, the over-exploitation of energy resources, and the rapidly warming climate are all combining to bring mounting pressure on the Earth's environment health."

This study, which was led by U.C. Berkeley biologist Anthony Bernosky, reported their analysis in the journal NATURE. In that report, the scientist say their research shows many combined factors are thrusting the world toward the tipping point they foresee. He proceeds toward this conclusion to explain several factors that will raise the global temperatures to a point much higher than once predicted. Within the next 60 years, the average global temperature will be higher than it has been since the human species evolved, he proclaims.

At this point the article becomes rather odd. Under a heading titled "Not a sure thing" and for the rest of the time, Perlman goes on to explain that there is "considerable uncertainty" that these forces will actually lead to such a rapid and radical transformation of the world's environment…a "state shift" as they call it. Yet…he argues such a shift is "highly plausible" and may have already begun. Really?

This is all very odd…to say the least. Even the way it was presented is strange. It is almost as if Editor Diaz felt it necessary to throw a bone to environmentalists and give them front page (above the fold) piece on "Global Warming". Which as a subject, has not been so popular lately.

After reading this article, it is just not likely that people in the Bay Area are going to feel any way about this subject, other then confused. To begin with, why do you think this editor felt it was necessary to place this rather obscure piece on the front page above the fold?

What was the ultimate goal here for Anthony Barnovsky? After all, he conducted the study and he was the researcher that ended up with this wholly confusing conclusion. Are we the readers expected to understand that after trying to digest two totally diverse conclusions, we should be clear on any part of this mess?

According to David Perlman, "slowing or reversing that transition will require international cooperation to slow population growth, curb dependence on fossil fuels, increase the efficiency of food production, and manage both lands and oceans as reservoirs of biodiversity". Yet…he also introduces us to Richard Lindzen, a climate scientist at Massachusetts Institute of Technology (MIT) who has been a "vociferous skeptic" on the urgency of global warming, calling the warming by Barnosky and his colleagues "highly implausible". Even if their models of the future were correct, what's crucial here is the time frame, and no one thinks that something terrible will happen in anything like the future they see…or will be a part of. According to Lindzen, "Their population predictions are extremely unlikely, and their climate predictions are always hypothetical".

No matter how often they publish or regardless of the intensity of their predictions…these scientists have yet to prove (without serious or continuous doubt) their validity or their accuracy. These doubts remain and will continue as long as there are truck size gaps in the research. It just doesn't happen to be true just because Anthony Barnovsky and his colleagues choose to believe it is. We, as a country, deserve to know what the real science is. So far… we have not seen this. What happened in Copenhagen in 2009 proved without a doubt that a great deal of what has been presented in the past as good science, simply has not been.

The content of that article and its particular location in the Chronicle were strange indeed, and need some sort of explanation on the part of the editor. But…don't look for that to happen, you and I do not come under the classification of "need to know". And… "Climate Change" is a very serious subject…or didn't you need to know that?

Fundraiser Supreme

The other day, Fox News Network announced that the president had attended 150 fundraisers in the last 14 months. WOW! That, it turns out, is more than all of the fundraisers combined by Presidents Clinton and George W. Bush during their two terms each in the White House.

Combine that with the 90 rounds of golf played by this president during the last three years and the question persists; when does this man have time to do what a President needs to do in order to run this Country properly?

In addition to the golf and the fundraiser is the matter of the 14 vacations. Not the usual presidental haunts mind you, such as Camp David and the Coast resorts of New England, but the exotics in Hawaii, Europe and Asia. Normal arithmetic would show that the Obamas have vacationed every ninety days since he was elected. One vacation taken alone by the First lady, and a plane load of friends to Spain, cost the taxpayer nearly 2 million dollars. The mount of money spent by this president has been, for the most part, nearly totally ignored by the national media. The shouting match last year between the president and his Chief Advisor, David Axelrod, in regard to the money the First Lady was spending on that trip, was totally ignored by the major media. If not for Fox News Network, it is highly doubtful that news of that red hot argument would have ever reached the general public.

The Obamas appear to think of themselves more as royalty than as public servants of the American people. The huge cost of flying around this country and abroad is totally ignored by the Press, and only when the First Family goes really overboard (there are more of these occurring than you could ever imagine) do we hear from the main stream media.

Such things as the "dates" the President has taken his wife on (New York, for instance) have been unbelievably expensive. Two huge Air Force planes, one for the President and his wife and guest, and one for his Secret Service and staff, have been so "over the top" expensive as to raise eyebrows around Washington and the rest of the Nation. Cost has never been a consideration according to sources close to the White Hiouse.

To those of you who say "all presidents spend too much ", my answer to you is: no they don't. None have been even close to this man. This President has spent more money on vacations, trips, and gifts than Presidents Clinton and G.W. Bush combined during the total time of their eight year terms.

It has been very difficult to write a political column about national politics during these last three and a half years without discussing the negative aspects of this President. It simply can't be denied that Barack Obama has been one of, if not the most, incompetent presidents this Nation has ever had to endure.

The track record produced by President Obama has been dismal...to be charitable. Nothing that he promised during his election campaign in 2008 and for the years that have followed, has come to fruition. In addition, this may just be the most mendacious President of all time. I have been accused by many of being too hard on Mr. Obama, but I have only stated the truth as it has happened.

It is very difficult for any President to promise everything to every one and not disappoint most. And..that is what this man has done starting during his campaign in 2008 and continuing to this day. It simply cannot be done and even as inexperienced as Mr. Obama was when elected, he certainly should have known that.

The major media in this Country should be mightily embarrassed about the way that they had coddled and protected this President, to the detriment of the Nation.

I have no apologies to make about the manner in which I have kept my readers informed of his in ability to run this Country. All I can do now is sit back and watch these last five months as they unfold and keep my fingers crossed that the American voter has discovered who this man really is. The question I asked nearly four years ago; "Who is Barack Obama?" has been answered. But...don't be surprised if his problems get even worse over the next few months. He simply must be defeated.

Craig Becker and the NLRB- 2012

In the year 2009- the first year of the Obama Administration, Andy Stern, since deposed president of the SEIU Labor Union, visited the Oval Office 44 times. You remember Mr. Stern don't you? He is the Andy Stern that the president spoke of in a taped speech to the Convention of the Union in which he said- "when I need to talk to someone in regard to the problems of working men and women of this country, I go to Andy Stern! When I need advice on how I should approach numerous serious problems involving the economy of this Country—I go to Andy Stern!"

During this speech to the Union membership, Obama repeated that same mantra 12 times. He did it with the emotion of a gospel tent preacher. He was riveting and obviously full of devoted fervor. "I am not a newcomer to this, I have spent my adult life working on behalf of this Union," he barked. In the spirit of that devotion, the president recently placed radical labor lawyer Craig Becker on the National Labor Relations Board (NLRB) by recess appointment. The same Board that is now suing the State of South Carolina on behalf of a Machinist Union at the Boeing Aircraft Corporation in Washington State. Now Becker is not only a radical labor attorney, he was also the top lawyer at the Service Employees International Union.

While working for the SEIU, Becker helped write three pro-labor executive orders that Obama signed just a week after taking office. The effect of the Stern influence on this president had already begun. An important milestone was reached last year when, for the first time, the majority of Union members (51.4 percent) were State or Federal Government employees. The political power of Government workers unions is a major reason why Government spending is now out of control. And an undeniable reason the State of California is nearly bankrupt at this time.

The average pay for Federal workers in Washington is now $94,047. Whereas the average pay in the private sector (providing you are working) is

$50,028. Annual raises are a matter of course, and Government employees enjoy close to lifetime job security and benefits that include retirement. In the last 18 months the number of Federal employees making $150,000 has doubled.

Another Washington lawyer, Joe Sandler, who is described as a "renowned expert on election law" has created a voracious gathering of front groups whose goal is to undermine the Tea Party movement. This bunch has funneled vast amounts of Union dues money, including $10 million from the American Federation of State, County, and Municipal Employees (AFSCME) into fronts with innocuous names such as "Patriot Majority" and "Citizens for Progress". To defeat proposition 8, the SEIU spent $500,000 and the California Teachers Union spent $1,250,000. After the voters approved the measure, over 50 Unions (including the AFL-CIO) signed a brief asking the Courts to overturn the will of the people.

Some of the prospective nominees who are reputed to be on Obama's short list for the next Supreme Court vacancy are weirdos of various flavors. One says it is OK for the Indiana Legislature to open with an invocation to Allah but not Jesus; another calls himself a transnationalist and wants to integrate foreign law into the U.S. domestic law. Another wants dogs to have lawyers and says the Government owns the organs in the body of any person who may die soon, and can remove them without any consent. I am not making this up folks. God help us.

It is an almost sure bet that Goodwin Liu, the young U.C. Berkeley Law School Dean and currently the newest member of the California Supreme Court, will be nominated and seated to fill the next open seat on the U.S. Supreme Court should a seat become available before November 2012. That will give Obama a leftist Supreme Court majority. Even the thought of that happening gives most Conservatives in this Country cold sweats at night. With a "progressive" Court at his bidding, Obama will surely uncork some ultra-liberal programs that would never pass muster in the Court, as it is presently configure. As a result, look for there to be some serious pressure on Justice Ginsburg to retire within the next 12 months.

This State is in unbelievable turmoil. A very large reason for this is out of control Government unions. There was a time in this Country when Labor Unions were the salvation of the working man. Because of Unions, pressure was brought on tyrannical corporations and American manufacturing to the point that the working man was finally afforded fair treatment and pay. That is no longer true and has not been for a very long time. If the truth were told, the majority of the blame for the near destruction of the American auto industry and most American heavy manufacturing should be place where it belongs…on the Unions. It is hard to say where all this is taking the State of California and us as individuals, but none if it will ever change as long as this State continues as a one Party enterprise.

This Country can be changed. California, however, is not so fortunate. Despite recent attempts to stop the gerrymandering of voting districts in the State by a citizen commission, both the State House and Senate will continue to be the hand maidens of the Democratic Party and Labor Unions. It is a pitiful situation that appears to have no solution other than the wholesale removal of the politicians that have put us here. God help us, no one else seems able to.

A Job for a Mental Therapist

What is happening in this country cannot be explained by anyone other than mental therapist. The platform for a Government-controlled society is being prepared with each new Government spending program. Once the American people have been convinced the Government should manage their jobs, the rest of the Socialist agenda will follow. My friends, we are in severe trouble and the vast majority of us have no idea how we got to this point. In the last eighteen months, this president and his party in Congress have increased our National debt to a number higher than was accumulated in the entire prior history of this country.

By this point, many are going through disappointment, and anger about what we have allowed these people to do to our Nation and especially to our future generations. But most of us didn't do it purposely, we simply bought the lie. We allowed ourselves to believe the lies that were told because it was just more convenient to do that rather than to take the liar to task.

Any thinking person with the conservative background of most Americans has to realize that on one, our Government included, can spend more than they make indefinitely. We certainly have had adequate warning from leaders of past generations. President Abraham Lincoln warned, "You cannot keep out of trouble by spending more than you earn". And Thomas Jefferson also warned, "To preserve our independence, we must not let our leaders load us with perpetual debt. I place economy among the first and most important of republican virtues, and public debt as the greatest of the dangers to be feared".

But Americans have allowed themselves to wallow in debt because it is better to create the debt than reduce their benefits. After all, Pogo said "We have met the enemy and it is us". The massive spending of the Government has spanned two Presidential administrations and defies belief. The Bush Administration was no small player in this debacle, but it pales in comparison to what Obama and his Democrat majorities have done.

If we were to add all the debt this country has acquired since the founding of the nation, it would not amount to the debt that this Congress has placed on this nation in the last 18 months. There is no possibility on God's green earth that we can ever balance this budget---ever---unless we stop spending. And yet this President continues to propose new spending programs that place every single tax payer and his children and their children in a debtor position from which they will never be able to extricate themselves.

As unbelievable as it appears, this president adheres to the old concept of "spending your way out of debt". Never been done—can't be done. Not by this president or any other Socialist leader in history. In Russia, this Socialist/Communist system failed and fell with the sound of thunder and lightning. China, after watching Taiwan trounce their economy, did the smart thing, they became a free enterprise nation and now trail only this country in GNP. The small Socialist Scandinavian nations of Sweden and Denmark or Norway, due to their size, are the only nations in the world where this system has survived. Size does matter when it comes to cradle to grave social systems.

But none of this matters a penny's worth to Barack Obama. During his apology trip to Europe last year, he was amazed to find nearly every European leader that he spoke to, counseled him to not make the mistakes in his economy that they had in the past in theirs. "Work toward balancing your budget and bolstering your economy" was the advice of the leaders of France, Germany and England.

He left Europe embarrassed and no longer so sure that he could will things done with his great oratory skills and bright smile. The juxtaposition was delicious. But, just recently, the exact same thing happened in Canada during the G20 Meeting at which Obama again attempted to convince the European powers that spending was the way to solve their recessionary problems. The results were exactly the same. The answer was "Surely Mr. Obama, you have got to be kidding, Sir". He was dead serious, but so were they.

What do you know about the 10ᵗʰ Amendment?

The 10ᵗʰ Amendment to the Constitution states: "The Powers not delegated to the United States by the Constitution, nor prohibited by it to the States, are reserved to the States respectively, or to the People."

Thomas Jefferson explained the pre-eminence of this amendment in 1791 when he stated: "I consider the foundation of the constitution as laid on this ground: That all powers not delegated to the United States, by the constitution, nor prohibited by it to the States, are reserved to the States or the people. To take a single step beyond the boundaries thus specially drawn around the powers of Congress, is to take possession of a boundless field of power, no longer susceptible of any definition."

Based on the 10ᵗʰ Amendment, when it comes to legislating and controlling our health care, the Federal Government doesn't have a constitutional leg to stand on. And this is rather odd given that our current president actually taught constitutional law a graduate student instructor.

Surely, if he taught it he should b aware that what the Congress is doing today in regard to health care is totally unconstitutional.

I challenge any attorney or law professor who happens to be reading this, to point out to me where in the Constitution it says that the Federal Government retains the right to control the health of American citizens and the states of this union do not. I would also ask where in the Constitution it says that the Federal Government can force a citizen to buy health insurance—or a quart of milk, for that matter?

Our 44ᵗʰ president would do well to learn from America's third president, Thomas Jefferson, himself a source greater than any living constitutional lawyer. In 1823, Jefferson wrote in a letter to Supreme Court Justice William Johnson: The States supposed that by their 10ᵗʰ amendment, they had secured themselves against constructive powers. They did not learn, nor were they aware of the slipperiness of the eels of the law. I ask for no straining of words against the General Government, nor yet against the States. I believe the States can best govern our home concerns, and the General Government our foreign ones. I wish, therefore. to see maintained that wholesome distribution of powers established by the Constitution for the limitation of both; and never to see all offices transferred to Washington, where, further withdrawn from the eyes of the people, they may more secretly be bought and sold at market.

Is this not what has been happening in the Senate lately (Ben Nelson)? Can anyone deny that the Senate was not "secretly bought and sold at market"?

Can anyone deny that both houses of Congress have been for sale to the highest bidder during the entire healthcare debacles?

What a pitiful display of arrogance and ignorance by our Congress. How sad and disheartening that this bunch is all we have. This is what it is. This year we have the opportunity to rid ourselves of most of the people we elected, thinking that they believed as we do. When you have the time, sit down and think about why you vote in the first place, and look around and judge just what that vote has gotten you.

Sad isn't it.

What Wisconsin Predicts

On June 5 of this year, the people of Wisconsin voted whether or not to recall their Governor Scott Walker. The Governor won the election in a land slide., the people of Wisconsin were not buying what the Unions were selling that day.

This recall, instigated by public-employee Unions, was the Union's way of protecting the Governor's hard won reforms that have saved the people of Wisconsin more than billion dollars. Prior to Walker's reforms, State and local Government employees paid nothing or very little toward their pension and paid only slightly more than 6 percent of their health care premiums.

According to the Wisconsin Taxpayers Alliance, the average Wisconsin Government employee earned $71,000 in total compensation in 2011, and were more than capable of sharing in some of the cost of these benefits.

The same year, average total compensation for employees of the State's largest school district, Milwaukee Public Schools, reached $101,091. Walker helped close the State's $3.6 billion deficit by requiring public employees to pay 5 percent of their salaries toward their pensions. He also required State employees to pay 12.6 percent of their health-insurance premiums....less than half the average both in the private sector and for Federal Government employees. No pain there.

In the end, less than 50 percent of Labor Union members (of all types) supported the Government Unions in this recall attempt. The president had been avoiding the State like a plague, and had not visited Wisconsin at all this year. The reason for this is simple: the Government Union members are not victims here. How does the President go to their rescue when there is nothing from which to rescue them?

Prior to Walker's law, all Government workers were required to join Unions and pay dues... and Unions were able to negotiate all conditions of employment...

wages, benefits, and work rules. Walker made Union membership optional, eliminated the automatic deduction of Union dues, and ended Collective Bargaining for everything but wages. And…for this the Government Unions propelled the State into chaos for a good part of 20112.

The Capital was occupied by, to steal a term by Mark Twain, the "great hive" of public employees, who banged drums, blew whistles and camped on the marble floors. Fourteen Democrat Senators fled the State for weeks to block a vote on the bill.

A Government-Employee Union issued a Press release comparing Walker to "Adolph Hitler", and someone turned a camel loose in the Capital square. But, in the end, it was not as effective as they had hoped it would be. The president was not confident that the Unions would win this election and…the president "does not need to associate with losers", explained David Axelrod, the president's former Chief of Staff, currently running his campaign from Chicago.

The Government Unions in Wisconsin were anything but confident and they continued to lose confidence by the day. The president had basically abandoned them (as he is prone to do in such matters). And fellow Union members did not come to their rescue…not this time. Let's face it folks.. this is not the same man that ran with such confidence in 2008. This is not the same man that stood in front of huge adoring crowds and offered "Hope and Change" for America. This time, we have a president that is running scared and he is not getting any better. What we got was "change" but this kind of change was not what we had "hoped" for.

If the Unions had won this recall it would have been a dark predictor of things to come. But, one could not imagine the people of Wisconsin (or America) falling for the "long con" once again. The people of Wisconsin were just too darn smart to go down that same road, (this time) with their eyes wide open. Wouldn't you think the president would have stopped just once during those flyovers the last few months…and that stop…(at the very least)..would have buoyed the spirits of the Unions toward the end of the campaign? But…as Mr. Axelrod explained… "the president is a very busy man these days". But after November?

A Serious Problem in America

This year our country witnessed the most ridiculous political series of party debates our system can recall. The candidates were "packaged" by cynical manipulators of the public's basest fears, "sound-bite zingers" were preferable to intelligent statements of position, image took precedent over issue. The presidential debates were neither presidential nor debates but canned Pavlovian responses more often than not having little or nothing to do with the questions.

The ground rules for the robotic pavanes were drawn up by glib intellectual misfits who thought so ill of their clients that they refused to allow them top speak more than two minutes!

The orators of the cradle of democracy, the ancient Athenians, wherever they are, can be heard crying. Perhaps one bright day in the future we will return to legitimate civilized campaigns, where an open exchange of ideas can be heard. Who knows? All that has been truly documented from time immemorial is that man continues to kill without needing the meat of his quarry, his politicians lie in order to avoid accountability or, conversely to seize the reins of accountability to such an extent the social contract between the government and the governed is theirs alone to write...they endlessly seek to enrich themselves at the expense of the public, and while he is at it, tries all too frequently to turn his personal morality or religion into everyone else's legality of religiosity, no quarter given to the unbelievers of pariah-dom. Good Lord, we could go on and on.

In 2008 this country was exposed to a series of faux events and the total mendacity of our current president during a presidential campaign that was unique only in the extraordinary amount of lies told. Today we are faced with phase two of the "Big Lie" Obama style. Our president has nothing to run on. He certainly cannot present his record of the last 40 months as something to be proud of. The Democrat Party is being forced to go on the offensive and attack his adversary constantly in order to keep the spotlight away from Mr. Obama as much as possible.

In the last two weeks, I visited several countries in Southern Europe during a wonderful cruise down the beautiful Danube. They included Germany, Austria, Slovakia, and Hungary. I was intent on talking to as many on the ship as possible about the American presidential election. I was pleasantly surprised to find so many highly intelligent individuals willing to give me their opinion of our country and particularly our president. Some of their answers surprised me and some did not. Over all, the country scored relatively high and the president did not.

We have to face the fact however, that most Europeans are not fond of Barack Obama. They have found him to be both arrogant and condescending. The president's attempt, as early as his first trip to European capitals in 2009, was ill received to put it mildly. European leaders were aghast at the temerity of this man to advise them on how to run their various economies. Some of those I spoke to, included a Swiss national with a strong opinion of this country. This gentleman was a retired travel expert and truly had the numbers and facts at his fingertips. He was convinced that the worldwide recession began in America, and had it been handled properly by this government, Europe would have been in much better shape today. He was not a happy camper (to put it mildly).

He was rather harsh in his appraisal of the president's ability to run this country. Given that the economy of Europe rises and falls on what is happening in America, when an American president fails to do his job, it effects all of Europe as well as the rest of the world. He was also upset wit the American Electorate's failure to see this inadequacy in Obama in 2008. "He was incompetent and your country and our countries have had to pay the price" he said in a calm and calculated statement.

The American dollar has, as a consequence of our debt, fallen to a level that makes traveling abroad very costly. As a result of that, countries that have depended greatly over the years on the American tourist industry have suffered greatly. And as a result of that…our government is not among the favorites in Europe. I find it interesting that the people of Europe are seeing all of this much more clearly than we are. It is very hard to convince ignorant people to vote the right way. Much to the chagrin of the people of Europe, Barrack Obama has not been beaten yet and if he is not, then you will see a very negative reaction abroad.

Inequality in America

The word being used more consistently lately than any other in politics is inequality. American civilization today has become more and more unbalanced between those that have and those that don't. Of course, has it ever been balanced? I mean really balanced in this country? Has it ever been truly balanced in any country in the world? Stop and think about that. The supposed goal of Socialist and Communist countries was supposed to have been the equal spreading of wealth, unfortunately, it didn't work in those countries either.

The fact is: There has always been a certain element of civilization that will continue to be underachievers regardless of the circumstances. We will never have a system that will guarantee that 100% of those capable of working, will want to do so. You could spread all the money in the world around to equalize the wealth of the earth on the first day of the year 2012 and by the first day of 2022, those who had been the richest before will be well on their way to being the richest again.

Fact number two: As long as these economic systems depend on the theory of equal pay for all regardless of effort expended, there will never be any incentive to work hard. There will never be any reason to do more and better than those that don't. There will never be any reason to want to do better than the next guy if there is no greater reward. That is human nature.

If you took every dime the top 1% of wage earners made in 2011 and gave it to the IRS, it would make not a small dent in the National debt. If you took all that money and spread it among the lowest wage earners in the country, it would amount to less than $1,000 per working person. The "redistribution of wealth" our pseudo/Socialist President speaks of, simply is not the answer to the problem folks!

What is needed by the average poor person in this country is not a handout, it is a job. There is however, a certain element that would be perfectly satisfied with that handout if it included a flat screen television set and a food stamp card. Thirty years ago, institutional forces still existed in politics, business, and the media that could still hold things together. It used to be called "the establishment", and it no longer exists. Solving fundamental problems with can-do practicality- the very thing the world used to associate with America, and that redeemed us from our vulgarity and arrogance- now seems beyond our reach.

Today, we have a president that distinctly despises these institutions to such a degree that shortly after his election, he took that dissatisfaction to Europe. To assure the rest of the world that he was not one of those vulgar, arrogant Americans, he took a shot at nearly everything that epitomized the greatness of his own country. The very attributes that have made us great were the ones he disparaged the most. In this election year, we should never allow him to forget that.

Our president is so enamored of European Socialism that he is willing to look right past its total failure over the last 20 years. Europe is in far worse shape economically than we are, yet this man continues to beat the socialist drum. There is no way that the America in which I was raised can be salvaged if we continue down the path we are on. But...we can start the process by electing a new President in 2012. When there is CHANGE there is HOPE!! I seem to remember something like that?.....well close.

Obama and the French

I can just picture the smile on our presidents' face when he learned the Socialist/communist candidate was now the new President of France. There is no question that Francois Hollande is openly one of the most far left politicians in Europe and ran on a ticket that Obama would comfortably have run on himself if he thought there was a chance he could be elected openly proposing a 75% tax on the rich, higher taxes on everyone, and even more extensive "cradle to grave" social programs in a country currently going through a severe recession.

That is what Mr. Hollande sold to the French…and they bought it. That would be amusing if it were not so totally absent any common sense. But then, the French have never been known for their commonsensical attitude. Just how the average French citizen could look around him and see what is happening to its' neighbors Greece, Spain and England, and not be aware of what Socialist programs can do to an economy, is a mystery to me.

Yet, it is actually easier to understand once you realize that we have a portion of our Society here in America that would be just as easy to convince. The same people who pay no taxes, who rely on our Government to pay the biggest portion of their rent (Section 8), and provide them with a credit card with which they pay for the majority of their groceries (EBT).

In addition, nearly all the cost of their medical needs are paid for by a city, county, state or Federal Government. When you think that all of this is currently provided right here in California to a large segment of our population. France, England and most Scandinavian countries don't seem so over the top any longer. California is indeed a Socialist State, whether we recognize it or not

And… it is exactly programs like these that have nearly bankrupted a great many European countries. All we have to do is look at the riots in the street all over Europe to be aware of what is in store for us her in our country. Yet, this is exactly what Barack Obama is proposing that his Government do to combat our current fiscal crisis.

He actually believes in, and has been trying to sell to the political leaders of Europe., the theory that they can spend their way out of debt. Try to do that as an individual and see where that gets you. It doesn't work for the individual and it will not work for this country. This is just one example of the failed leadership of this President.

This is a President who simply refuses to seek another way to keep his country from falling into the abyss. But folks…we are not France. We have not been exposed to this overt "cradle to grave" Socialist theory as have the Europeans. All we need is a new leader with sufficient brain power and the backbone to "just say no".

The similarities between the French and American Presidential elections are many, and both incumbents suffer with border problems. According to the Washington Times, "With demonstrations, riots, and governments falling like dominoes, Europe's ruling elites are losing the confidence of the people and its ruling parties are bleeding support to the more militant left and right. Both the French and American borders no longer function properly, if at all'. In France, new inhabitants whose first language is not French, are poring into the country in mass numbers. The cost of these people is overwhelming the French nation. We, in this country, are very aware of that dynamic. We are in the same boat.

What does this portend for France? Probably an easing up of austerity… of the tax hikes and budget cuts for payrolls, pensions, and health care- all things demanded by Hollande during the campaign.

The French populous appears to have won this one, to the detriment of France and the European Union. One would hope that the people of this country keep a close eye on what happens in Europe. Our future depends on it.

Our "Constitutional" Lawyer/President

Look out folks! One of the most dramatic and important U.S. Supreme Court decisions in the last 100 years is nearly upon us. Sometime in the next sixty days or so, the Court is going to give us their decision on "OBAMACARE". And…according to most Constitutional scholars around the country, the Court is going to (at least) find the "individual mandate" section of the bill to be unconstitutional. Actually, there are also many of these same scholars who feel that it is possible that they may throw out the entire bill!

The fact that the man behind this bill (Obama) is referred to by the major media as a "Constitutional" Law Professor would lead one to believe that he certainly should know a constitutionally proper bill when he sees one, and would have been particularly certain that this bill met the "Constitutional" standard, don't you think? Well, it appears that he didn't. Presidential contempt for the Supreme Court and inconvenient law is not new. But rarely has a president sounded so uninformed as when Obama lectured the Justices on what they can and cannot do to his cherished Obamacare.

The Court, would take an "unprecedented and extraordinary step" if it overturns his healthcare scheme because it was enacted by a "strong majority of a democratically elected Congress", the president declared. Obamacare actually cleared the House by only 219 to 212, and on their face the president's remarks betray an astonishing ignorance of the Constitution and how the Republic works.

The President, who frequently describes himself (inaccurately) as a former Professor of Constitutional Law, sounded willfully ignorant. The White House has been putting out "clarifications" every day since, arguing that Mr. Obama, once a "Senior Lecturer" at the University of Chicago Law School didn't actually say what he actually did say. Hello, what was that?

At this point, it becomes increasingly interesting. According to those who should be closest to this President, Mr. Obama's rant was not meant for Republican politicians, pundits, lawyers, and academics. He was talking to his congregation and his choir, building a fire under them and giving an advance look at talking points for the campaign to come if the Court kills or wounds Obamacare. He is more willing to sound dumb and ignorant in the greater cause for his re-election.

The President's rant against the Court was in line with the race baiting tragedy in the death of Trayvon Martin. Instead of quietly assigning the Justice Department to determine the facts and whether Trayvon Martin's Civil Rights in Federal law were violated, the president suggested the tragedy was all about race when there is no evidence that it was about race at all.

Race baiting, ugly but often effective, was once the exclusive province of the Right. It has become now the default tactic of the Left. Mr. Obama used the tactic skillfully. He put his remarks about the Trayvon Martin tragedy in the most calculated and emotional terms… "if I had a son, he would look like Trayvon Martin"… and his lecture to the Supreme Court was carefully calculated, and appeared to look like he was determined to be precise and specific. The later "clarification" put out by the White House, however, retracted nothing.

Attorney General Eric Holder delivered at the end of that remarkable week, the "three page, single spaced letter" requested by the U.S. Appeals Court Judge in Houston. It was affirming that the Justice Department agrees, even if the President appeared not to, that the "power of the Courts to review the Constitutionality Legislation is beyond dispute". No surprise there, and we can be sure that the President vetted the letter, heck, he might even have written it himself.

One outraged pundit even decided that Mr. Obama had revealed himself to be "no longer a serious man, nor an honest one". This misses the point, too. Barack never was …honest, that is.

A Practiced Form of Deceit

I assume all readers of this column are aware of polite society's (and our lovely communities) favorite theory of "climate change". According to this theory, anthropogenic (once known as 'man made') gases waft into the atmosphere, causing worldwide catastrophes and our imminent doom. But how many of you are familiar with my new theory? According to it, our culture is polluted by political ideas, prejudices and false pieties advocated by the liberals or progressives or people of conscience or whatever the devil they are calling themselves nowadays. They keep changing designations, and every designation they opt for becomes an honorific, at least to them. Liberals, indeed…they actually favor government coercion and regimentation (although they don't recognize it as that). Progressives, indeed…they are for a political system that was recognized as archaic in the last century, when socialism was found to be obsolete even in Russia and China.

Recently, in the Forum, one of Benicia's highly respected authorities on "Climate Change" expressed to us her true love and respect for former Vice President Albert Gore regarding his huge new book on the globalization of the earth's economy. Yet anyone who was alive and able to read and/or comprehend the English language in 2009, is surely aware of the total debunking of most of Mr. Gore's theories on global warming. During that time nearly all of Mr. Gore's theories were put to the test and found lacking one critical element: the unassailable glow of truth. Today Albert Gore is continuing to fabricate and to sell other forms of Voodoo Science, this time involving the world economy. Trust me folks…if Albert Gore is recommending any sort of involvement in any program…please hold onto your wallet.

Less than four years ago, hackers, (I like to think of them as selfless public-spirited hackers) Broke into the electronic files of one of the leading global warmist research centers, the Climatic Research Unit of the University of Anglia in the UK, and posted 3,000 conspiratorial e-mails for all the world to see. To my ineffable gratification, the e-mails displayed the global warmist sedulously engaging in just what you would expect: deceits, distortions, and the suppression of dissenting points of view. Here we had a comprehensive view of my theory in the making.

Our friends in the editorial sanctum of the Wall Street Journal pored over all the damning e-mails. They found dissenting scientist (global warming skeptics, as they are called) being black listed and suppressed. For instance, Michael Mann, Director of the Earth System Science Center at Penn State University, e-mailed like-minded global warmist advising them to isolate and ignore scientific journals that publish the views of skeptics. "I think we have to stop considering "Climate Research" as a legitimate peer-reviewed journal", he wrote, going on to urge the encouragement of his 'colleagues' in the research community to "no longer submit, or cite papers in, this journal". Now that is how you classically taint any debate.

Then there is the case of Phil Jones, Director of the University of East Anglia Project. He e-mailed Mann and asked him to "delete any e-mails he may have had with Keith" regarding another e-mail from Jones to a co-conspirator asked that he change the received date! "Don't give those skeptics something to amuse themselves with". The Journal also quotes an unnamed scientist e-mail that said to "hide the decline" of temperature in data that might cast a doubt on global warming. Well…I can understand. In fact, since 2004 there has been no global warming, contrary to the global warmist computer predictions!

Never Let a Good Crisis Go to Waste

President Obama has said that he misses being anonymous. Well... he sure was on the budget bill, wasn't he? Usually, our president runs off on vacation when things get tough. Had the Democrats won this last election, Obama might be a happier person spending his heart out and claiming the social compact is more important than the budget. The president knows that he squandered away the first two years of his term on Obamacare and I think he has been told so by his party, especially those who lost their seats in the House and the Senate. But ... it's true.

I keep telling myself, and all those that will listen, that I can't believe that he can win another term. BUT...ON SECOND THOUGHT, he is likely to take both California and New York on the basis of simply being a Democrat. That said, a Republican candidate will have to take 20 states in order to get the same amount of electoral votes. He could win because some Democrats will vote for him no matter how bad things are going in this country. These voters are clueless and gullible and a great many are instructed to do so by their Labor Unions.

He will convince this group that it was the Republicans that stood in his way regardless of the fact that he had complete control of all three branches of the Government that created that debt over the same two year period.

As incompetent as I believe this President to be, I do not underestimate him. The American people are not really tuned in because they are constantly being manipulated by the media. Someone like Donald Trump pops up and people begin to take notice and listen. Why do you think Huckabee has a TV show? It is to keep Obamas' face in front of the camera. I want Obama to be anonymous again, nothing could please me more. But then again, it seems that every time the man opens his mouth, he puts a foot in it. The President has been an unmitigated disaster for anyone with sense enough to be objective about his job performance. The only ones who still believe rare the ones who are so deep in the Kool Aid that they no longer are in touch with reality.

In the words of Rahm Emanuel… "Never let a good crisis go to waste". Obama's whole term has been a crisis and a waste.

Goodwin Liu Revisited

Today, the Associated Press announced that Goodwin Liu, a professor of law a U.C. Berkeley, has been nominated for the California Supreme Court. Anyone that has been following my previous columns on Mr. Liu is aware that I do not hold Mr. Liu in high regard as it pertains to his qualifications to sit on any appeals court.

He simply is not qualified. Goodwin Liu has never been a judge of any court. He has practiced law a grand total of 21 months and has zero litigation experience. The young man just turned forty and was actually nominated to sit on the Ninth Federal Court of Appeals in San Francisco at the age of 37.

The left leaning Associated Press reported that the reason his nomination was blocked by Republicans was due to his writing, which included his support of reparations and other radical stances on immigration. It was also stated that Mr. Liu was too inexperienced to do the job.

I am puzzled as to why we have this constant attempt by progressives in this country (and this state) to place this man on some appeals court. Why Goodwin Liu? Why not some other candidate with less baggage and more credentials? This consistent effort to get this man on an appeals court.... any appeals court. It is an affront to common sense. If we were to look at this as a first step toward placing him on the Ninth Court of Appeals (second attempt), even that would seem scurrilous upon close examination.

Jerry Brown makes no attempt to explain why he feels this appointment should be considered as the best he has at this time. There are a multitude of possible candidates in this state that are much more qualified than Liu. Brown appears flippant when he states that he has no litmus test for judicial appointments. About opinions on the death penalty, gay marriage, and other hot button issues...? I expect he will "follow the law," Brown is reported to have said.

The Governor is also quoted as saying that Liu's lack of experience will add to the diversity of the California Court, where the six sitting judges all served on lower courts before their appointments. The six are Republican appointees. Is it me or does that sound like a senior moment from Mr. Brown? How far down in the candidate barrel does he think he has to go to find a candidate left enough to suit him? The State is simply chocked full of leftist judges that actually have experienced being a judge.

In regard to the Republican criticism of Liu's inexperience, aroma tells us "I don't think that should be given a lot of intellectual weight". Really? I don't think there is a large number of intelligent people in California who feel that anything said by Brown should be given any intellectual weight. Does anyone remember "Governor Moonbeam".

Let's face it folks. There is no way that Goodwin Liu will not be seated on the California Supreme Court. It will come to pass. The people who will make the decision are: Chief Justice Tani Cantil-Sakauye, Attorney General Kama Harris, and Court of Appeal Justice Dempsey Klein.

Regardless of the fact that this appointment will remove the only Hispanic influence on the court, Brown's answer to that… "I don't think people should be appointed because of natural origin". But, this appointment will remove all Southern California representation on the court. Somehow, I don't think that bothers Jerry at all.

Come Hell or High Water

According to *Foreign Policy Magazine, "Forget Russian, these days its Barack Obama who is the proverbial riddle wrapped in a mystery, inside a n enigma". In regard to government controlled and operated healthcare in this county, no one has ever managed to present more confusion and elevated ill feeling more than our President. And even a man of unmatched vocal ability such as Mr. Obama is lost when trying to navigate in the fog of this dilemma.*

Make no mistake, I am not attempting to present Mr. Obama in any way other than as a man dedicated to his dreams of all Americans acquiring proper health care. That part is easy…everything else is do murky as to be nearly without explanation. It is hard providing 30 million people in this country coverage they currently do not have, without raising taxes on all of the rest of us. It is a question he or anyone else, seem to be to unable to answer.

Actually, the answer is fairly simple… there is no answer! We don't have the ability to provide the kind of money necessary to make that possible without borrowing more money from China. And yet, the President and the Democratic Party keep coming at us ad nausea with plan after plan that the people of this country simply do not want. It seems to make no difference to this man that this country lacks the financial credibility and the moral necessity to shove this thing through…come hell or high water.

For over 24 months Obama was in front of the cameras, in front of the microphones, talking up *his* health plan. *Today he says that "it appears that I simply did not explain my plan properly". Yes, you did Mr. President, you have explained it over and over again. We know what it is and we don't want it and cannot afford it. Enough already, sir!*

He has told the majority of this country (73%) that he was going to pass that bill (whether they liked it or not). Such arrogance by a President has never been seen in this country before now. He said in that short speech that he was not concerned about the politics of that thing...really? He exclaimed that people needed it and he was going to give them (some version) of healthcare, and let the chips fall where they may.

2013 OVERVIEW
In the Beginning There Was Democracy

The current spending spree and escalation of our national deficit to record levels by this Congress, cannot be explained by anyone other than a political science professor or a mental therapist. But, what is evident is this platform for a new government-controlled society is being strengthened with each of these current government spending sprees.

And once the American people have been convinced the government should manage their lives, the rest of the Socialist agenda will follow. My friends, we are in severe trouble,

and the vast majority of us have no idea just how bad it is or how we go to this point.

In the last eighteen months, this president and his party in Congress have increased our national debt to a number higher than was accumulated in the entire prior history of this country.

By this point, many of us are going through disappointment, despair, and anger about what we have allowed these people to do to our nation and especially to our future generations. But most of us didn't realize what was happening. We simply bought the lie. We allowed ourselves to believe the lies that were told because it was just more convenient to do that rather than take the liar to task.

Any thinking person with the conservative background of most Americans has to realize that no one, our government included, can spend more than they make indefinitely. We certainly have had adequate warning from leaders of past generations. President Abraham Lincoln warned, "You cannot keep out of trouble by spending more than you earn". And Thomas Jefferson also warned "To preserve our independence, we must not let our leaders load us with perpetual debt. I place economy among the first and most important of Republican virtues, and public debt as the greatest of the dangers to be feared".

But Americans have allowed themselves to wallow in debt because it is better to create the debt than reduce the benefit. After all, Pogo said "We have met the enemy and it is us". The massive spending of this government has spanned two presidential administrations and defies belief. The Bush Administration was no small player in this debacle, but it pales in comparison to what Mr. Obama and his Democrat majorities have done in the last 18 months.

If we were to add all the debt this country has acquired since the founding of the nation, it would not amount to the debt that this Congress has placed on this nation since this President took office. There is no possibility on God's green earth that we can ever balance this budget--- ever---unless we stop spending. And yet this President continues to propose new spending programs that place every single taxpayer and his children and their children in a debtor position from which they will never be able to extricate themselves.

As unbelievable as it appears, this president adheres to the old concept of "spending your way out of debt". Never been done---can't be done. Not by this President or any other Socialist leader in history. In Russia, the Socialist/ Communist system failed and fell with the sound of thunder and applause. China, after watching Taiwan trounce its economy, did the smart thing, they became a free enterprise nation and now trail only this country in GNP. The small Socialist Scandinavian nations of Sweden, Denmark and Norway, due to their size, are the only nations in the world where this system has survived successfully in its basic form. Size does matter when it comes to cradle to grave Socialist systems.

But none of this matters a penny's worth to this president. During his apology trip to Europe last year, he was amazed to find that nearly every European leader that he spoke to, counseled him to not make the mistakes in his economy that they had made in theirs. "Work toward balancing your budget and bolstering your economy" was the advice of the leaders of France, Germany and England. He left Europe no longer sure he could will things done with only his oratory skills and bright smile. The juxtaposition was delicious.

But just recently, the exact same thing happened in Canada where during the G20 meeting, Obama once again attempted to convince the European powers that spending was the way to solve their recessionary problems, The results were exactly the same, When Sandra Merkle of Germany responded: "Surely Mr. Obama, you cannot be serious, Sir." He was dead serious, but so was she.

The simple fact is this: If we continue to spend at the rate we are spending now, and this administration is allowed six more years in office, we will be well on our way to becoming a third world banana republic. You may disagree, but there is just no other result possible, The people in this state and in this nation have to start paying attention to what is really happening in Washington and less to the rhetoric of this man currently sitting in the Oval Office. The choice is ours, but not for long.

2013 List

Veterans Day... 2013

Looking back today Veterans' Day, 2013, I am reminded of an issue of "Foreign Policy" magazine not so long ago in which Harvard professor Stephen Walt and New Times political columnist Thomas Friedman provide their readership with a couple of very interesting articles in which they do their absolute best to disparage America. For the life of me, I cannot understand how intelligent supposedly patriotic citizens of this country can participate in this sort if very nasty behavior.

Even here in lovely little Benicia, there are supposedly intelligent men and women who write regularly in the same manner as Professor Walt and Mr. Friedman. They are learned individuals whose life experience has led them in a different direction from this humble writer. They are fervent in their opinion, but they are more often wrong than right.

Both of these men (Walt and Friedman) have provided in these "Foreign Policy" articles and examples that are hard to refute. This country has not always behaved as a "shining light" on the world, and those two do point out some less than glorious periods in our history. We have expanded our power and our political philosophy throughout the world, and we have done this numerous times without different systems which they apparently accepted.

We, as a country, are not without serious blemishes. We have (in our self righteous attempt to remake the rest of the world in our image), made some serious mistakes. At the same time however, we have done much more good than not. We have brought democracy and personal freedom to dozens of countries around the world that would never have experienced the fresh air of freedom without us. Ours is a good country with a continuous goal of doing more good than evil for other nations.

We have never set out with a goal of expanding our power in an empirical way. Empire has never been the goal of this nation. But, if you read these two men closely, you will see a continuous attempt to put America in a bad light. Continuous and with intent.

I personally have very little respect for either of these men, even though I must give them credit for making some clearly viable points in these articles. Yes, we have made mistakes and errors that have sometimes put us in a bad light around the world. We have done this in the process of becoming the most powerful country in history. And…that is one great big daddy of a responsibility folks. I doubt that either of these men could name one nation that has performed so well, carrying that sort of responsibility. Perhaps Rome comes closest, but surely it had its faults too, there is no denying that. Its downfall came from within. The erosion of Roman power started with the decay of its moral responsibilities (sound familiar)? Great Britain basically ruled the world for well over a hundred years. For the most part it was generous in its rule, but not always.

In the end, both of these men conceded somewhat to the conclusion that no other country in history has ever done it better. For both it was sort of a painful admission that despite all of the pimples, this is the greatest nation on earth and of all time. Now someone should explain that to Barack Obama, (who does not appear to understand this).

No mention was made in either article of his embarrassing "apology" tour of Europe in which he denigrated his own nation while he praised European political leadership and used Europe as an example of the way we should be handling our economy. Given that Europe is actually in worse financial shape than we are, that performance left an awful lot of Americans very angry as well as puzzled.

What this country needs, and quickly, is a leader who actually leads. Not one who gives speeches and points a finger at others when what he does fails. One thing for sure, we don't have one sitting in the Oval Office today. There is a long list of progressive political writers that continuously find fault with this country, but curiously very seldom with its present leadership.

These writers, which include columnists such as Hendrick Hertzberg at the New Yorker magazine, Joe Cline at Time, Friedman at the New York Times and Foreign Policy.com. These men are on a continuous crusade to make sure all America knows what a rotten bunch we are.

I, for one, had just about enough of this nonsense, I am willing to bet the farm that neither of these characters would give up his citizenship in order to live in another country. Most of all of these men are products if Ivy League East Coast universities where they were taught from early on that Europe was the Mecca of political thought during the last half century. Socialism has been the "shining star" of political science courses in these institutions of higher learning. Our college students have been misled for over fifty years by some men and women lecturers in our universities to believe our system of government should be subservient to socialism. That is wrong. These academics are just plain wrong. A very bright light needs to be put on these teachers and universities. The most troublesome aspect of this is that this group is teaching opinion as if it were fact.

The celebration of "Veterans' Day" was designed to celebrate those men and women who have put their lives on the line to protect the citizens of this country from those who would take away our freedom and rights. One only has to look at the writing of these two men to realize that it is of no particular consequence to them.

Some Things Never End

At the age of 16 and just a year before the end of the "Korean Conflict", I joined the newly formed U.S. Marine Corps Reserve Unit in Charleston, SC. That was 58 years ago and since, there has never been anything other than a cease fire at the border of South and North Korea. This war was never declared over and yet we still have over 30,000 troops on the ground on that border.

This is something that simply has not gone away. And today it has become a real thorn in the side of world peace. Frankly, I have no idea why this thing had not been declared over and done with and why we had not pulled our people out of there. Today, I think I have a better idea. It isn't pretty, but it may be just the only thing we are left with.

We have a little lunatic running North Korea who has used the existence of his million man army to threaten peace in the whole Far East for longer than I can remember. We have allowed this man to blackmail us and the rest of the world for years. Every president in the last 40 years has simply thrown him a bone when he puffed up his chest and threatened war. It is a duck and dodge strategy that has been used by four presidents and doesn't appear likely to change anytime soon.

Now if the truth were known, should North Korea actually seriously attack the South, they would be soundly defeated and the whole world, (but mostly the U.S. and China) would be stuck with an entire nation hardly able to feed itself. It is exactly the reason this has been going on for 60 years.

The recent artillery attack on the island Yeonpyeong was the first on a civilian area since the fighting stopped in 1953. Diplomats have been running around like crazy attempting to diffuse regional tension and Beijing has called for an emergency meeting between chief delegates to long stalled six-party talks on the North's nuclear disarmament.

What our State Department has known for a very long time is that North Korea, should it engage in a ground war with the South (and most assuredly

American forces), simply could not support its troops for more than a few months. Its reserve of hardware and daily supplies simply doesn't exist They never have.

It has taken nearly 70% of North Korea's food and clothing resources just to feed and provide uniforms and necessary supplies to its army. That is the reason that its civilian population is, for the mot part, unfed and improperly clothed at this time.

It is generally believed that the North has nuclear capability. It has little else in the form of a war machine other than a hungry million man army with antiquated weaponry that would be more a liability than an asset during a conflict. During the Korean war, the combined forces of South Korea and the United Nations handled the North Korean army easily and was putting a severe beating on them up until the Chinese entered the fray.

Once the U.N. forces regrouped after the Chinese insertion, it was only a matter of time before North Korea sued for a cease fire. And here we are. In the South, we have one of the top economies in the world, and the original aggressor in the so called "conflict" sits to the North in constant need of food to feed its people. It does, however, have a leader that has had 100 holes in one in golf and who once bowled the score of 300 five times in one night!

Everything about North Korea over the last five decades has been a sham and a huge con game. The people of the North have suffered terrible hunger and freezing winters as well as being treated as basically slaves to a Social Dictatorship that may be the worst in the world. Surely there is some way that the combined countries of this planet can remove this man from power without having to drop a bomb on him (And unfortunately his people as well.)

This administration has not shown any great skill in international diplomacy and appears to be going down the same appeasement road as all its predecessors. The prognosis of anything happening at this time is not encouraging. We will give Kim Jong-11 whatever he wants and he will stop doing whatever he has been doing in order to get it.

Some things never end.

Activist Journalism

My loyal readers are quite aware that I try to keep up to date on the activities of those journalists in this country that persist in writing un-American and un-ethical material on anything that might shine a bad light on out nation.

On August 18th, security officers at London's Heathrow Airport detained a Brazilian named David Miranda. They did so under the United Kingdom's Terrorism Act which allows authorities to hold an individual for up to nine hours if they believe him to be in possession of information which he believes might be of "material assistance" to terrorists.

Miranda is the partner of The Guardian journalist Glenn Greenwald, who since June has broken a series of stories about programs conducted by the National Agency and other intelligence services, all based upon leaks from former NSA contractor Edward Snowden. One such program, Prism, enables the NSA to gather from international companies. Greenwald also revealed the existence of a top secret order that gave the agency access to telephone record log, or metadata" from Verizon.

Greenwald and others portrayed these legal programs in Orwellian terms, writing of sinister "mass surveillance", as if every human being on earth's phone calls and e-mails were being overheard and read by analysts.

Many other journalists and activists were quick to accept the line that Miranda had been targeted as a result of his relationship to Greenwald. Not so, according to Oliver Robbins, British Deputy National Security Advisor, who told a court two weeks later that Miranda had been in possession of roughly 58,000 classified UK intelligence documents, "a large proportion" of which are "either secret or top secret". The "disclosure of the material could put the lives of British intelligence agents or their families at risk", Robbins wrote and "the general public could be also endangered if details about the intelligence operations or method fell into the wrong hands".

If patriotism has become "old days", the last refuge of scoundrels in our post national wired world, then treason has become the sign of the truly independent thinker. Such figures are beholden to no state. Examine the way, for instance, that Greenwald selectively views the disclosure of classified information, particularly the identities of undercover agents. It was long ago that Greenwald and many of the same people now praising as a "whistle blower" were calling for the heads of those individuals they believed had revealed the name of the CIA officer: Valerie Plame.

Contrast Greenwald's contempt for those who leaked the identity of Plame with his reaction to the plight of Raymond Davis, the CIA contractor who fired a diplomatic crisis with Pakistan in 2011 after shooting two men dead in Lahore, Davis claimed the men had acted in self defense. Washington insisted that Davis was a State Department employee and protected by diplomatic immunity, a claim it would later have to retract after The Guardian irresponsibly revealed his true identity.

While actively supporting (in words and materially) the work of American traitors, Greenwald simultaneously accused American friends of Israel of putting the interest of the Jewish State before their own. "Not even our Constitution's First Amendment has been a match for the endless exploitation of American policy. Law and resources (by the Israel) to target and punish Israel's enemies", he wrote a few years ago.

The Pelosi Rebellion

As I write this today there is a very unusual situation taking place in Washington. Former House Speaker Nancy Pelosi is facing a growing number of rank and file that say they will not support her for minority leader in a symbolic roll call when the new Congress meets in January.

In addition, there is a wrestling match going on between Rep. Steny Hoyer of Maryland, currently the No 1 Democrat and Rep. James Clyburn of South Carolina, the number 3. The two are competing for the second in command position in the minority in a contest that has taken on racial overtones in recent days with the decision of the Congressional Black Caucus to endorse Clyburn.

Reading about Jim Clyburn takes me back many years ago to when Mr. Clyburn was running for a seat in the South Carolina House of Representatives. Clyburn was a Charleston City Councilman and his district was heavily African-American and his opponent was also African-American. During that race he was alleged to have committed voter fraud (his staff was accused of registering dead people for the election).

It was pretty much an open and shut case for the Solicitor (District Attorney) Jim Condon. There were numerous witnesses who swore under oath that the Clyburn group had committed untold acts of fraud at Clyburn's direction during the campaign. So Mr. Condon went to trial very confident. James Condon is now Attorney General of South Carolina, and I can assure you, remembers this case very well.

Little did Condon know he would be prosecuting Clyburn three times and would do no better than a hung jury in each. There were at least 2 African-American jurors on each jury and in each trial, both of these seated jurors would not change their 'innocent of all charges' verdicts. Condon was absolutely determined to convict Clyburn, but this was a classic case of 'jury nullification' and after three attempts he simply gave it up.

What is even more interesting is that following those trials, many years later, Condon attempted to take another African-American candidate (Robert Ford) to trial for exactly the same charges and ran into exactly the same result. Mr. Ford has been a sitting member of the SC House of Representatives now and for over 20 years. Having these memories fresh in my mind, every time I see James Clyburn on camera standing behind Pelosi along with George Miller, it sends me scampering for an antacid. Sometimes crime does pay. In this case…absolutely.

Democratic officials say Pelosi has urged the aforementioned Mr. Clyburn to bow out of the race and run for a lesser leadership job, with an additional promise of a newly created face-saving position on a key committee. The officials spoke on condition of anonymity, saying they we not authorized to discuss private discussions.

Hoyer is widely viewed as the voice of moderate Democrats in the leadership, although his list of public supporters include powerful liberals. Ole Jim is now the most powerful African-American in Congress. Many Democrats are eager for a smooth transition and make note that if Pelosi were to withdraw, it would smooth a face-0off between Hoyer and Clyburn.

One would assume that the Congressional Black Caucus would not be so enthused about backing Clyburn if they knew about his trials in Charleston….or wouldn't they? The rumor in Charleston is that Robert Ford is planning on running for the Clyburn seat in 2012. Now wouldn't that be a hoot? There ought to be some form of justice in there somewhere. Maybe not.

In the meantime, it appears that Pelosi will succeed in her bid to become the Minority Leader. It is necessary to note however, that her imperial action of naming herself to the job was arrogant at best and the reaction could have been predicted. The queen appears to have lost her crown, but not her hubris.

And the Voodoo Beat Goes On

With over 6 trillion dollars already spent during his tenure, you might think that the wild drunken spending of other people's money (that we do not have) is President Obama's single greatest talent. It turns out that there is something else that he is even better at.

That would be the hysterical doom and gloom fear mongering we have witnessed these past weeks over comparatively small cuts to the Federal Government. Mr. Obama's terrorist threats have been amply noted everywhere. Planes falling from the skies, starvation in the streets, teachers being sent home.

What is truly astonishing about this is not all of the dire and reckless predictions he has made. Nor is it that already many of his predictions have proven to be demonstrably false. And…nor is it that he has so clearly orchestrated a widespread and deceitful campaign to punish Americans with real pain over the cuts to the Federal Government their lawmakers have allowed to happen. What is truly astonishing and breathtaking here is that all of this doom and gloom Mr. Obama has predicted appears to be precisely what he wants for this country.

To put this all in some sort of perspective: No one can continue to assert that the president is simply incompetent. But, of course, he is indeed that. Into his fifth year as president, America is worse off than ever before and millions are unemployed….those numbers stand exactly where they were the day he took office, and millions more are on food tamps than ever before…and, despite his claim otherwise, the U.S. is less respected in the world than before he took office.

But that was all before the sequesters. The order trims every dollar spent by the Federal Government…read: your money…by a paltry 2 cents. To understand the enormity of the cut, consider this: the 2013 budget calls for 3,603 billion dollars in spending now, with the across the board automatic cuts, the government can spend 3,518 billion. Who is fooling who here? Just curious. During President Carter's first year in office, it soared to $409 billion. President Reagan, in the midst of the Cold War, continued the deficient spending. By 1987, expenditures topped $1 trillion for the first time. Under President George W. Bush, the budget soared $2 trillion. And in 2009, the budget went from$2.9 trillion to $3.5 trillion. Estimates show that cash outlay will top $4 trillion just two years from now.

There is little merit in arguments against spending cuts, and not a speck of support for the theory that America can tax itself out of its growing sinkhole. The Federal Government simply has grown too large, and spends too much. We are now borrowing 35 cents of every dollar we spend. Like any family faced with a shortfall of cash, the first…..and really, only solution is to reduce spending. It is not rocket science. And Americans are doing jus that every single day.

So with all the doom and gloom, what did the president do? Did he seek to sooth America, allay its citizens' fear of Armegedon? How about saying, "Hey, you are tightening your belt; the least your government can do is cut spending"? Quite the contrary. The president has spent the past few weeks needling up the horrors that will come from cutting a scant 2 cents from every federal dollar spent. America will be less safe, parks will shut down, food will not be inspected, illegal aliens will run freely, and the elderly will die unattended…the list went on and on.

Republicans offered the president a chance to make his own cuts. Democrats in the Senate, no doubt at his direction, rejected the bill. And it was this president himself who devised the automatic budget cuts, even though he claims the Republicans are solely to blame. Rush Limbaugh has been saying for months that it was the president who was not the least bit interested in the welfare of the country. Instead, he wants to kill the Republican Party for good. And he is right, folks. Last week's intranscience makes it clear. Republicans were ready to negotiate: Not on taxes, House Speaker John Boehner said, but on how…and who…the coming cuts will hit. The president didn't budge.

But there is more. The last thing he cares about is the plight of American families. American citizens have become Mr. Obama's Voodoo Dolls and he is jabbing them all over with sharp pins and placing demonic hexes on them as you read this. He wants us to feel the pain and to associate that pain with the leaner government espoused by his political opponents. No, the president wants to gut the Republican Party so he can win back a majority in Congress in 2014 and secure his legacy. He is fully prepared to spur chaos to get what he wants. When lawmakers were engaged in fierce, partisan negotiations, the president could have said: "I see this as a huge opportunity, and it's being squandered by politics, by the people who are more interested in a political victory than they are in doing what is right for this country". But he didn't…and the Voodoo beat goes on.

Janet Who?

What is going on with airline security in the world today? Could anyone possibly be unaware that this young Nigerian, who attempted to blow up a Northwest Airline flight into Detroit recently, bought his ticket with cash, boarded without luggage, and was neither red-flagged nor screened or body searched?

When he boarded his flight in Amsterdam, he did so without a passport or documents of any kind! That was a Dutch no-no, but had he succeeded it would have been this country that suffered the consequences. What on God's earth were the Dutch thinking about? Out State Department must absolutely come down on them like ton of bricks, but don't look for it to happen.

Simply put, the world today is not in fear of, nor have respect for the United States of America. Nor should they, given the administration now in the White House. We have a president much more interested in going to war with the Fox News Network than with al-qaeda, the Muslim Brotherhood, or any other terrorist group.

Don't get me wrong…I am not saying that Barack Obama is not capable of taking on these terrorist groups, what I am saying is he appears not to be particularly interested in doing so with any enthusiasm or haste. Either he is conflicted by some strange moral or religious issue or he is simply incompetent, or surrounded by incompetents in his administration.

A prime example of this incompetence is our Homeland Security Secretary who appears to be totally incapable of handling situations such as this attempted airliner bombing. What could possibly have prompted our president to nominate, or the Senate to confirm, this woman (Janet Napolitano) with absolutely no prior experience in international security? Being the Governor of Arizona simply cannot prepare one to take on the security of the United States. Given that Phoenix leads the nation in alien kidnapping cases, it appears Janet was not even prepared to handle the job there. God help us!

In Detroit, we were spared the horrible consequences of our incompetence, only because of the bomber's incompetence. The episode raises the questions not only about airline security, but about how we are fighting the real war we are in.

America and the Kennedy Phenomena

Whatever bargain Joe Kennedy struck with the devil, the expiation of it was cruel. The poor man was forced to watch his three sons precede him to the grave and left to die in the knowledge that Teddy would succeed him as head of the family. That surely could not have pleased Joseph Kennedy Sr.

Given old Joe this much. It is not every guy whom the devil finds it worth his while to tempt with gifts of fame, fortune, and a dynastic legacy. However, the Kennedy family arrived at our doorstep precisely at the right time in the right place. And…Washington was never to be the same place again.

For the truth be known…I am not so sure that we were prepared for John Kennedy, any more than he was prepared for what was to be the legend of Camelot. I never understood myself just what the legend was. Truly, he was unique…unlike most all of his predecessors…he appeared to promise something the nation was craving. And when he was murdered (for certainly it was that) what the people were looking for…was simply never identified.

O course, which of us is ever certain that he was ever capable of meeting the standard that this nation had place on him. He never accomplished anything particularly spectacular while he lived…and yet it is easy for one to imagine all the things he could have done had he not been taken from us at such an early age, without the chance to thrill us with his achievements or the promises of greater things to come.

Alas it is a spurious dream. The reality from which it diverts us is found in the neighborhoods in which we actually live. Kennedy played a part in this ongoing nationalization of consciousness. He was the first television president….his cult was as unthinkable as that of our current president. There is more in a TV cult like Kennedy's or Obama's than a whiff of Roman decadence. Both of these men beguiled the people not only with gifts, but with shows, and shows no less than gifts, eventually got the best of them.

In the case of Barack Obama. He will live to face the inevitable. All the answers to all questions asked will one day come forth and we will see the man as he really is and has been…all along. We will never know however, what marvelous things John F. Kennedy could have, perhaps would have, done for his country. Something tells me it would have been a serious, honest effort, if not Nirvana. Historians in time will tell us just what they think about Barack Obamas's legacy or lack thereof. Something tells me he will not be pleased.

With John F. Kennedy…anything was possible at the time. Mr, Kennedy never promised us anything other than what he thought just might be possible in a land where possibilities are always with us. It was …as always… up to us to make those possibilities a reality. He was the handsome young leader of a team on which anything was always possible.

Compared with the current resident in the White House…Kennedy was the real flesh and blood leader for which this country continues to dream. He was not the messiah nor did he ever pretend to be. We suffered a tremendous loss on that fateful day in Dallas, for on that day, we lost a real possibility of finding the leader that we must find in order to hold this nation together. Perhaps he is out there waiting to be discovered. There are quite a few highly qualified men in this country. Men who do not have to create the Wizard's curtain in order to sell us on the dream.

Perhaps we will find that man (or that woman) one day. Let us hope so, for surely we are in desperate need and no one seems to be on the horizon who does not hold before him the pot of gold which he assumes so many are looking for. That man was never Barack Obama., He simply never has had the brilliant abilities necessary to make that dream come true. With young Jack Kennedy…those abilities were present..but not the time. How sad is that?

For all general purposes, this presidency is finished. Mr. Obama simply has used up all of his assets and has little or no clout with Congress.

And…don't look for that to improve folks. The anchor to his legacy….
Obamacare…is dead in the water, with little or no chance of recovery. Even
as a result of some minor miracle…and the Democratic Party manages to
salvage the Senate in October 2014, there is simply nothing upon which he
can build a legacy. Mr. Obama thought he could create a pseudo socialist
economy and government upon lies and untruths. He could not. Even
John Kennedy with all his charm and popularity could not have pulled
off that scam. Mr. Obama has often been compared with JFK….but
the American public knew John (no one can claim to know who Barack
Obama really is) but by now they also know that Barack Obama is not
John F. Kennedy. That you can bet on.

An open letter to our President

Recently (Dec. 2013) in an issue in the Washington Times, the Times ran a stringent "Open Letter" to the president regarding his "overreach and abuse of power, and his inability to protect the People of the United States." This article, which covered a full page, was chock full of eye-opening facts which very few Americans were aware.

Titled as a "Dear John" letter to House Speaker John Boehner, the article went on to chronicle a laundry list of actions taken by this president that clearly were over-steps of his presidential authority. The article stated that it was up to the Speaker to stop this president's "out of control abuse of power which included Mr. Obama's broken promise of having the moist transparent of all administrations when he uses executive power he does not possess to conceal every iota of his past including his fabricated White House birth certificate and his phony Social security and Selective Service cards."

The article ask the question "can a president refuse to enforce laws he ideologically disagrees with? The truth is…he can not. His oath of office requires him to uphold all of the laws of the United States." Can the president amend laws by Executive Order if he disagrees with them or if they aren't working for him the way he needs them to? "The separation of powers denies the Executive any legislative power. He can't pass a law. He can't change a law. And Executive Orders have no Constitutional standing as law."

Given how often this president has totally disregarded those facts in the past, one is prompted to believe that he is not likely to change in the future. In addition, it appears that given the fact that he actually taught "Constitution Law" at the University of Chicago (as a part time lecturer) his education in constitutional law at Harvard surely must have left something to be desired. The Washington Times went on to ask: "Where was your indignation Mr. Speaker when this uber-president, on a whim, began changing the provisions of Obamacare by Fiat? Is it not the speaker's job to be the People's check and balance against runaway tyranny?" My question is this…What does Congress do when this president decides that his power is limitless? What does Congress do when the president thinks that he can overrule it arbitrarily? Create a resolution for disapproval? Or kill the funding? Well…this president ignores the resolutions and takes the money to fund his agenda from some other program.

When it comes to our prosperity, our freedom traditions, and our constitutional government, President Barack Obama has been a one man wrecking ball…constantly knocking down the free-market economy and principles of limited government that have made America the envy of the world.

The Obama administration has waged a relentless, nearly five year long war to transform our nation into a country where federal-bureaucrats have more power over our lives than we do. Where, in an Orwellian version of meaning, a savagely weakened national defense somehow makes us stronger and trillions in deficit spending on counterproductive government "stimulus" and welfare programs somehow makes us richer.

And …let's face it folks…Obamacare is essentially a Socialistic Mandatory entitlement that reduces our personal freedoms and burdens our businesses so that it harms our economy. This entire health plan was predicated on the notion that if enough young healthy people in the country were obligated and required to purchase expensive health insurance they didn't need, so that 20-30 million people who were uninsured would be able to purchase coverage.

The only problem with that was getting the young and healthy to buy the insurance. So far…they can't or they will not. And today wee are looking at far more people who have lost their original coverage than those that have been able to get new policies. A net negative situation, no doubt about it. And…how many average Americans do you think are aware of all this… or even care?

Today, my wife and I got a phone call that stated that the government wanted to give us $3,000 worth of food coupons and a free Emergency Medical alert. All for just signing up for the program and being 65 or over. No other requirements, and this was entirely unsolicited folks! You wonder why we are in the terrible shape we are in? Wake up…it is not going to get any better anytime soon.

The President's Effort to Reconstruct our Government

This nation stands basically transformed. We are no longer a democracy (in the strictest definition of the word). America today has been fractured into two different nations: The tax producers and the tax consumers. The givers and the takers, those who generate wealth and those that exploit it.

The productive classes have been harnessed into subsidizing the non-productive elements. Statism and gender trumps entrepreneurship and self reliance. Contrary to myth, liberalism is not a political ideology, but a pseudo-religion...or rather it is a substitute, irrationality, and blind intense faith. Its Holy Trinity is race, class and gender. Its church is the Democratic Party and its savior....its secular messiah... is Barack Obama.

He has fostered a cult of personality common among leftist revolutionaries. Despite blatant failures, he is not held responsible by his supported. Like Lenin, Trotsky, Castro, or Hugo Chavez, Mr. Obama is never blamed by his constituencies such as unions, public sector workers, environmentalists, African-Americans, and feminists. He is not blamed by his followers for any mistakes or misdeeds. It is always someone else's fault...especially the Republican Party, and George Bush, who happens to be the devil himself to the American left.

From the outset of his presidency, Mr. Obama vowed to be a "transformative" leader. His re-election shows that he has achieved his primary goal: erecting a European socialist democracy. By any objective measure his first term has been a colossal failure. His signature legislative achievement...the economic stimulus and Obamacare...have been by any measure extremely unpopular and in the case of Obamacare, a total train wreck.

Unemployment has remained chronically high and economic growth is sputtering. The recovery is anemic and inflation is beginning to rise noticeably. He has resided over multiple, consecutive trillion dollar budget deficits. He has amassed over $7 trillion in debt and the national debt has risen above the $17 trillion mark...a staggering amount that threatens our economic stability. We are sliding toward a Greece-like failure and impending bankruptcy. Yet we reward Mr. Obama with another term? Why? The answer is simple and ominous: because over half the population...50 percent plus one now depend upon government benefits. Over the last four years, Mr. Obama has created a Franco-German welfare state, whose sole purpose is to forge a majority coalition wedded to the Democratic Party. Given the results of the election, Mr. Obama is exactly the kind of leader a large segment of this country is looking for.

For the life of me, I can't understand how a man with such a total record of failure was ever re-elected president for second term. On second thought, just a minimum of research shows that this faction (that re-elected the president) was the same group that stood to gain the most from his re-election.

The stimulus, the healthcare overhaul, the redirecting of financial resources to the inner cities, the explosion in the number of Americans on food stamps and welfare, and the massive spending increases on public education, are just a fraction of the actions this president has taken to create his own personal fiefdom. Mr. Obama has created his own voting block....guaranteed to approve anything he proposes, just so long as those proposals give them what they want with a minimum of effort on their part. Now I am not talking about the elderly on Social Security here...nor college kids taking out tuition loans. I am talking about serial partakers of the "free lunch" that David Axelrod created to keep the president in office.

The path had been clear in the past for this president's complete transformation of America...that is up until recently, when the Healthcare debacle began to create a rather large road block. Until recently, he has admitted that the key to his latest election was the huge Hispanic turnout. The New York Times reported that Mr. Obama considered "comprehensive immigration reform" to be his first priority until the "Healthcare.com" debacle showed that he had some clearly more defined problems to consider.

Up to just recently, the establishment media has been his lap-dog. Almost every media institution had covered him with a positive blanket. Today we are seeing a different show. There is every indication that there are enough intelligent, reasonable individuals in this nation to halt this march toward the total secular-socialist state that Mr. Obama seems to crave. One thing is for certain: Barack Obama is not longer a "Teflon" president. This nation has awoken to the fact that he has "feel of clay" after all.

Enlightenment and Despotism

According to Mark Steyn at National Review Magazine recently: "For the last half century, Barack Obama has simply had to be. Just being Obama was enough to waft him onwards and upwards: He was the Harvard Law Review president who never published a word, the Community Organizer who never organized a thing, the State legislator who voted 'present'. And then one day came the day when it wasn't enough simply to be. For the first time in his life, he had to do. He is not Steve Jobs or Bill Gates. And Heathcare.com is about what you would expect if you nationalized a sixth of the economy and gave it to the Assistant Deputy Commissar of the Department of Paperwork and the Under-Regulator-General of the Bureau of Compliance."

No thoughtful American could possibly be a fan of the railroaded Obamacare bill crafted like Frankenstein's monster by House Minority Leader (our own wonderful Nancy Pelosi) in her quivering moment of glory. Launched against her own countrymen in the dead of night and wrapped in the haughty regalia of self-proclaimed ignorance (and with the compassion of a nest of cobras). Mrs. Pelosi and her accomplices stuffed a societal death sentence down the American throat.

History will indeed record this act as the signature of a president who succeeded in transforming America from the "evil" empire he imagined it, to be something else. But, President Obama is taking us from the exemplar of freedom through out the world to a sniveling nanny state in which there are no superlatives on true morality and no urge for individual achievement. Isn't it profoundly sad that we have allowed this to happen on our watch. Mr. Obama and his confederates have succeeded in plowing us toward the most Pyrrhic of victories. It was to be his crowning achievement. "How simple it is to roll the weak-kneed Republican establishment!" (they think.) Indeed the old guard is inept and has lost both its understanding of the central themes of our republic and its will to join the battle for American survival. There are a few Patrick Henrys out there. Other would be patriots are in hiding, rationalizing. They would have never stood on Bunker Hull.

What are 'We the People' to do? The answer is simple: Ignore blocking the appropriate hearings. It is within your power to do so. Amass the evidence of wrongdoing, forcefully bring those results to the public attention and begin impeachment proceedings. Because, first and fore most you have two responsibilities as the third most powerful man in America. Protect the Constitution of the United States from the overreach and abuse of power, and protect the people of the United States of America." That is pretty heavy wordage for one of the most read newspapers in the country.

I have over the last year written several columns in which I have rather severely castigated Speaker Boehner in regard to his failure to present a viable and strong position as it regards the Republican Party. What the Republican Party has failed to do is to actually perform as a realistic party of the opposition. John Boehner has laid down to the Democrats in almost every way over the last five years as both minority leader and Speaker. Even with a hefty majority in the House, Boehner has consistently allowed Mr. Obama to dictate the terms of conciliation on more than one occasion.

Today, the Speaker openly attacked the Tea Party organization as a destabilizing faction of the republican Party. This has finally brought to a head the constant bickering between the two largest factions of the GOP. One thing is for sure…it nearly seals the fate of John Boehner as leader of the party in the House of Representatives. It is highly unlikely that Boehner will be elected Speaker again should the GOP retain the House in 2014.

Almost from the beginning of his tenure, Boehner has had his detractors who have attacked his inability to deal with the president on any level. The man simply appears weak in almost every regard. (the tears don't help). Most importantly, his open animosity toward that branch of the party (Tea Party) which actually produced the huge Republican victory in 2010 and made him speaker, has in reality made him the weakest Speaker in decades from either party.

Folks….the Republican Party is on the brink of total collapse unless it finds its core. (and thus its strength). It will never regain its former position as the party of the opposition if it does not find a leader and its direction. In the meantime, I have declared myself officially an Independent,

The Spotlight Needs to Be on China

The upcoming meeting between President Obama and Chinese President Hu Jintao has given this country the opportunity to shine a light on just where we stand in the eyes of the world. According to the Wall Street Journal, the Chinese President has called the U.S. dollar functioning as the global currency a "product of the past" and is encouraging the global community to move toward the Chinese yuan for international investment.

This is a surprise to anyone? The handwriting has been on the wall for years. And if you throw in George Soros, a man responsible for bringing down four major currencies around the world including the British sterling and the Russian ruble, the situation gets even more scary. And folks, Mr. Soros is very much behind the scenes in Washington at this time.

A country's strength is in its productivity. Productivity and self sufficiency have become dirty words to many Americans. The U.S. has been sending its "productivity" overseas for years in the name of "free trade". Obama is so worried about the world and so hates our own exceptionalism that he fails to see how we are viewed through foreign eyes. And that is not a pretty site.

The 25 gun salute and other over the top treatment of Hu this week, will inevitably be viewed by the Chinese as kowtowing. It is at the very least accommodation and what exactly the distinction is between the two, I am not sure.

If we wind up incessantly accommodating China's aggressive behavior, it is almost certainly going to be construed by them as acts of appeasement. And there is a clear link between their economic leverage and their military expansion. Few American or International experts on China have any doubt it has a strategy for supplanting the United States as the pre-eminent power the world.

China's indifference, or actual encouragement of intellectual property theft and patent infringement, combined with a seriously undervalued currency, causes friction with American interest as well. The fact that China is pursuing "financial warfare" on the United States is very hard to refute.

In regard to the military strength of the two nations, the United States spends five times as much for hardware and other military cost as China or any other nation in the world. The actual size of the multi-million man army of China is of no consequence in this day and age. Any war fought between the two nations will be fought in the air and with the push of buttons. At this time, China is still not on the same technical level as the United States and should such a war begin tomorrow, China would be defeated. However, should America continue to allow China to steal military technology at the rate it is doing at this time, all bets are off.

The Chinese are aware of this and absolutely believe that they can defeat this country at the market place and they may be right. If this President allows Hu and/or any other Chinese leader to continually undermine our economy as they have been doing for the last decade, then folks, we are in serious trouble.

We will fall without the firing of a single shot. Should at anytime our President bow or even attempts to bow to this Chinese leader during his stay in Washington, then he should be sent home for good in 2012. Enough is enough Mr. President.

Printed in the United States
By Bookmasters